BEIJING'S
IMPERIAL PALACE

The Illustrated Guide to the Architecture, History,
and Splendor of the Forbidden City

BY YANG ZHIGANG

Reader's
Digest

The Reader's Digest Association, Inc.
Pleasantville, New York / Montreal / Sydney

FOR SHANGHAI PRESS & PUBLISHING DEVELOPMENT COMPANY
President and Publisher: Wang Youbu
Editorial Director: Wu Ying
Editors: Jennifer Wilde, Yang Xinci
Assistant Editor: Yao Feng

Text by Yang Zhigang
Photographs by Yang Zhigang and Wang Lixiang
Translation by Zhang Weiliang

Cover Design: Wang Wei
Interior Design: Yuan Yinchang, Li Jing, Xia Wei
Cover Image: Quanjing

Library of Congress Cataloging-in-Publication Data

Yang, Zhigang.
[You fang gu gong. English]
Beijing's Imperial Palace : the illustrated guide to the architecture, history and splendor of the Forbidden City / Yang Zhigang.
    p. cm.
ISBN 978-1-60652-121-2
1. Forbidden City (Beijing, China) 2. Forbidden City (Beijing, China)--Pictorial works. 3. Palaces--China--Beijing. 4. Palaces--China--Beijing--Pictorial works. I. Title.
DS795.8.F67W3613 2009
951'.156--dc22

FOR READER'S DIGEST
Executive Editor, Trade Publishing: Dolores York

THE READER'S DIGEST ASSOCIATION, INC.
President and Chief Executive Officer: Mary Berner
President of Asia Pacific: Paul Heath
President and Publisher, U.S. Trade Publishing: Harold Clarke

Printed in China by Shanghai Donnelley Printing Co. Ltd.

1 3 5 7 9 10 8 6 4 2

CONTENTS

A Historic Symphony of Joys and Sorrows

Maps

CONTENTS

A Bird's Eye View of the Imperial Palace (founded in the early 15th century, renovated and expanded several times, with the original layout remaining unchanged)

Introduction

At the heart of the city of Beijing is an imperial palace, largest in scale and best-preserved in state, amongst all those in present-day China. This is the Forbidden City of yesterday and the world-famed Imperial Palace of today.

This city within the city, surrounded by a 50-meter-wide moat and a 10-meter-high city wall, has an area of 720,000 square meters and served as imperial palace for both the Ming and Qing Dynasties. The entire architectural layout features the concept of the supremacy of imperial authority. The middle part of the palace is the largest and tallest, with the rest of the architectural structures extending out symmetrically from the central axis to form a unified completeness.

Tai He Dian (the Hall of Supreme Harmony), Zhong He Dian (the Hall of Central Harmony) and Bao He Dian (the Hall of Preserving Harmony) along the central axis and Wen Hua Dian (the Hall of Literary Brilliance) and Wu Ying Dian (the Hall of Martial Valor) on either side of the axis used to be locations where the emperors of both the Ming and Qing Dynasties held court, attending to political and state affairs. These halls constitute what is known as the Outer Court. To the north of the Outer Court are inner courts, also known as the Rear Chambers, which, including Qian Qing Gong (the Palace of Heavenly Purity), Jiao Tai Dian (the Hall of Union), Kun Ning Gong (the Palace of Earthly Tranquility), the Imperial Garden, and the Six Eastern Palaces and the Six Western Palaces along the central axis, form what is regarded as the emperor's home. "Front court, rear home" reflects a system of rites established in the early Qin Dynasty and handed down for several thousand years.

It is not easy to truly picture the power and supremacy of an emperor without seeing first hand the glory of the imperial home. The Forbidden City is magnificent, grandiose and orderly. Its entire design not only embodies the best of China's traditional culture and art, but also reveals the strong desire of China's emperors in the Ming and Qing Dynasties to wield power over the Heavenly Kingdom. The Hall of Supreme Harmony, a front hall of the Three Grand Halls, is where emperors used to perform important ceremonies. This accounts for its architectural feature of being the greatest in size, height and magnificence, a symbol of an emperor of absolute authority and power under the will of Heaven. The Hall of Supreme Harmony was the tallest architectural structure in the Ming and Qing Dynasties, with a height of 35.05 meters. This hall at the heart of the palace is accompanied and highlighted by buildings of diverse designs on its right and left, and to its front and rear. Looking over the Forbidden City from above, one sees red walls mounted with yellow tiles, shining splendidly bright, and palaces upon palaces with courtyard walls rising and falling in graceful disorder. All of these reflect the sacredness and mystery of the authority of an emperor.

The Imperial Palace was first constructed from the fourth year to the 18th year of the Yongle Empire (1406–1420), and has thereafter undergone repeated repairs and renovations. Some of the architectural structures have been several times reconstructed and have witnessed human sorrows and joys for as long as 600 years. After the Revolution of 1911, part of the Imperial Palace was made into an Antique Exhibition Hall. In 1924, the ousted last emperor Aisin-Gioro Puyi was expelled out of the Palace, and a year later, the Palace Museum officially came into being. In 1987, the Palace Museum was declared a UNESCO World Heritage Site.

The Imperial Palace has hosted 24 emperors throughout its history, who, together with their subjects and royal family members, have written numerous soul-stirring and heart-quaking epics, leaving behind a plethora of interesting and affecting anecdotes. This enclosed palatial complex was used by the emperors as their own personal kingdom, off-limits for the common people, while still in close contact with the outside world. It was known as the nerve centre of the Ming and

Qing Empires. The Forbidden City has experienced great changes and diverse hardships. It has paid witness to all the glories and splendors of the past empires, and recorded the incompetence and degeneracy of the rulers in the former days, and all the humiliations exercised upon the nation.

When you are strolling about the Forbidden City in the sunset, in the gentle breeze, in the morning fog, or in the chill wind, can't you hear it pouring out to you its own complex of stories?

This booklet is designed to serve as a guide on your tour of the Imperial Palace and as an introduction to its history and the culture which created it. This tour starts from Tian An Men (the Gate of Heavenly Peace) in the south, goes northward through Wu Men (the Meridian Gate) and concludes at Tai He Men (the Gate of Supreme Harmony) before a close view of the Three Grand Halls: the Hall of Supreme Harmony, the Hall of Central Harmony and the Hall of Preserving Harmony; and the Three Rear Palaces: the Palace of Heavenly Purity, the Hall of Union, the Palace of Earthly Tranquility. Then we shall tour Yang Xin Dian (the Hall of Mental Cultivation), the Six Western Palaces, Feng Xian Dian (the Hall for Ancestral Worship) and the Six Eastern Palaces along the two sides, and walk from the Imperial Garden, pass Shun Zhen Men (the Gate of Pursuit of Truth) and Shen Wu Men (the Gate of Divine Prowess) and take in a final view of the palace from the top of Jing Shan (Jing Hill or Scenic Hill).

The Imperial Palace today is the largest integrated museum in China, justified in taking pride in its more than one million rare collections. Pei Wenzhong, the late anthropologist and archeologist, said, "Both the Forbidden City itself in terms of its architectural complexes, and the cultural relics it has collected, are rare treasures without equal over generations." The majority of the collections of the Palace Museum were handed down from the palaces of the Ming and Qing Dynasties, and have witnessed the ancient culture and imperial power politics of China's history.

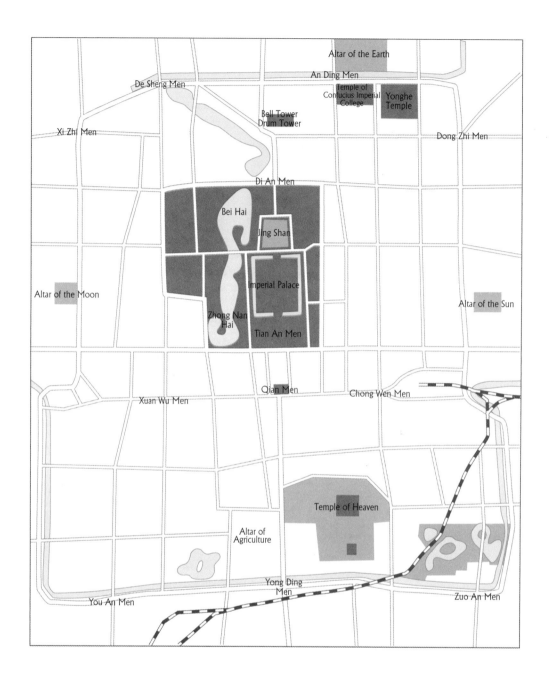

Legend of Imperial Palace and Other Tourist Sites

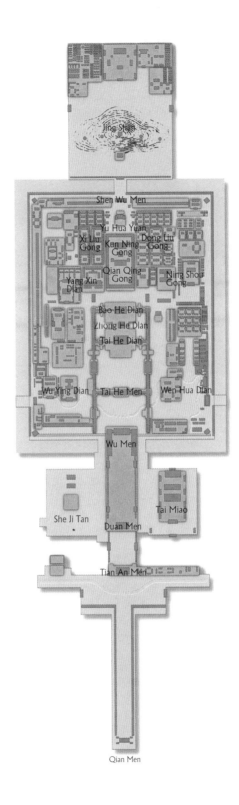

Jing Shan

Shen Wu Men

Yu Hua Yuan

Xi Liu Gong   Kun Ning Gong   Dong Liu Gong

Qian Qing Gong

Yang Xin Dian   Ning Shou Gong

Bao He Dian

Zhong He Dian

Tai He Dian

Wu Ying Dian   Tai He Men   Wen Hua Dian

Wu Men

She Ji Tan   Tai Miao

Duan Men

Tian An Men

Qian Men

Plan of Imperial Palace

Translation of Place Names in This Book

English	Chinese Pinyin	Chinese
Altar of Agriculture	Xian Nong Tan	先农坛
Altar of Land and Grain	She Ji Tan	社稷坛
Altar of the Earth	Di Tan	地坛
Altar of the Moon	Yue Tan	月坛
Altar of the Sun	Ri Tan	日坛
Bell Tower	Zhong Lou	钟楼
Belvedere of Crimson Snow Flakes	Jiang Xue Xuan	绛雪轩
Belvedere of Well-nourished Harmony	Yi He Xuan	颐和轩
Bridge for Royals	Wang Gong Qiao	王公桥
Bridge of Imperial Way	Yu Lu Qiao	御路桥
Building for Viewing Performances	Yue Shi Lou	阅是楼
Common Bridge	Gong Sheng Qiao	公生桥
Dominating Hill (Zhen Hill, Longevity Hill)	Wan Sui Shan (Zhen Shan)	万岁山（镇山）
Drum Tower	Gu Lou	鼓楼
Due South Gate (Front Gate)	Zheng Yang Men (Qian Men)	正阳门（前门）
Dui Xiu Hill (Hill of Accumulated Elegance)	Dui Xiu Shan	堆秀山
Eastern Warm Chamber	Dong Nuan Ge	东暖阁
East Long Passage	Dong Tong Zi	东筒子
Eastern Gate of Peace	Dong An Men	东安门
Eastern Prosperity Gate	Dong Hua Men	东华门
Eastern Swan-goose Wing Tower	Dong Yan Chi Lou	东雁翅楼
Five Phoenix Tower (Swan-goose Wing Tower)	Wu Feng Lou (Yan Chi Lou)	五凤楼（雁翅楼）
Front Gate (Due South Gate)	Qian Men (Zheng Yang Men)	前门（正阳门）
Garden of Exhilarating Spring	Chang Chun Yuan	畅春园
Gate for Ancestral Worship	Feng Xian Men	奉先门
Gate of Amiability	Xi He Men	熙和门
Gate of Benevolence and Auspiciousness	Ren Xiang Men	仁祥门
Gate of China (Great Ming Gate, Great Qing Gate)	Zhong Hua Men (Da Ming Men, Da Qing Men)	中华门（大明门、大清门）
Gate of Divine Prowess	Shen Wu Men	神武门
Gate of Earthly Peace (Northern Gate of Peace)	Di An Men (Bei An Men)	地安门（北安门）
Gate of Earthly Tranquility	Kun Ning Men	坤宁门
Gate of Eternal Settlement	Yong Ding Men	永定门
Gate of Faith	Zhen Shun Men	贞顺门
Gate of Fidelity	Zhen Du Men	贞度门
Gate of Genbu	Xuan Wu Men	玄武门
Gate of Glorifying Forebears	Long Zong Men	隆宗门
Gate of Great Fortune	Jing Yun Men	景运门
Gate of Heavenly Peace	Tian An Men	天安门
Gate of Heavenly Purity	Qian Qing Men	乾清门

English	Chinese Pinyin	Chinese
Gate of Initiating Good Luck	Qi Xiang Men	启祥门
Gate of Luminous Moon	Yue Hua Men	月华门
Gate of Manifest Virtue	Zhao De Men	昭德门
Gate of Mental Cultivation	Yang Xin Men	养心门
Gate of Obeying Morality and Justice	Zun Yi Men	遵义门
Gate of Promoting Literature	Chong Wen Men	崇文门
Gate of Promoting Martial Valor	Xuan Wu Men	宣武门
Gate of Pursuit of Truth	Shun Zhen Men	顺贞门
Gate of Spreading Happiness	Yan Qi Men	衍祺门
Gate of Stability	An Ding Men	安定门
Gate of Supreme Harmony	Tai He Men	太和门
Gate of Thriving Royal House	Xi Qing Men	锡庆门
Gate of Tranquility and Longevity	Ning Shou Men	宁寿门
Gate of Unified Harmony	Xie He Men	协和门
Gate of Uprightness	Duan Men	端门
Gate of Victory	De Sheng Men	得胜门
Golden River Bridge (Golden Water Bridge)	Jin Shui Qiao	金水桥
Golden Water Bridge (Golden River Bridge)	Jin Shui Qiao	金水桥
Golden Water River	Jin Shui He	金水河
Great Ming Gate (Great Qing Gate, Gate of China)	Da Ming Men (Da Qing Men, Zhong Hua Men)	大明门（大清门、中华门）
Great Qing Gate (Great Ming Gate, Gate of China)	Da Qing Men (Da Ming Men, Zhong Hua Men)	大清门（大明门、中华门）
Hall for Abstinence	Zhai Gong	斋宫
Hall for Ancestral Worship	Feng Xian Dian	奉先殿
Hall of Administering Supremacy	Jian Ji Dian	建极殿
Hall of Adoration	Chong Jing Dian	崇敬殿
Hall of Auspicious Swallow	Yan Xi Tang	燕喜堂
Hall of Canopy	Hua Gai Dian	华盖殿
Hall of Central Harmony	Zhong He Dian	中和殿
Hall of Central Supremacy	Zhong Ji Dian	中极殿
Hall of Imperial Peace	Qin An Dian	钦安殿
Hall of Imperial Supremacy	Huang Ji Dian	皇极殿
Hall of Joyful Longevity	Le Shou Tang	乐寿堂
Hall of Literary Brilliance	Wen Hua Dian	文华殿
Hall of Literary Elegance	Chi Zao Tang	摛藻堂
Hall of Martial Valor	Wu Ying Dian	武英殿
Hall of Manifest Mercy	Zhao Ren Dian	昭仁殿
Hall of Mental Cultivation	Yang Xin Dian	养心殿
Hall of Offering Heaven	Feng Tian Dian	奉天殿
Hall of Practising Moral Culture	Jin Shen Dian	谨身殿
Hall of Preserving Harmony	Bao He Dian	保和殿

Translation of Place Names in This Book

English	Chinese Pinyin	Chinese
Hall of Promoting Virtue	Hong De Dian	弘德殿
Hall of Spiritual Cultivation	Yang Xing Dian	养性殿
Hall of State Harmony	Ti He Dian	体和殿
Hall of State Satisfaction	Ti Shun Tang	体顺堂
Hall of State Unity	Ti Yuan Dian	体元殿
Hall of Supreme Harmony	Tai He Dian	太和殿
Hall of Supreme Principle	Tai Ji Dian	太极殿
Hall of Union	Jiao Tai Dian	交泰殿
Heavenly Gate	Cheng Tian Men	承天门
High-rank Bridge	Pin Ji Qiao	品级桥
Hill of Accumulated Elegance (Dui Xiu Hill)	Dui Xiu Shan	堆秀山
Imperial Ancestral Temple	Tai Miao	太庙
Imperial College	Guo Zi Jian	国子监
Imperial Garden	Yu Hua Yuan	御花园
Imperial Prospect Pavilion	Yu Jing Ting	御景亭
Jade Belt River	Yu Dai He	玉带河
Jing Hill (Scenic Hill)	Jing Shan	景山
Katydid Gate	Zhong Si Men	螽斯门
Left Gate of Chang An	Chang An Zuo Men	长安左门
Left Gate of Peace	Zuo An Men	左安门
Lodge for Proper Places and Cultivation of Things	Wei Yu Zhai	位育斋
Lodge of Fresh Fragrance	Shu Fang Zhai	漱芳斋
Longevity Hill (Dominating Hill, Zhen Hill)	Wan Sui Shan (Zhen Shan)	万岁山（镇山）
Meridian Gate	Wu Men	午门
Ministry of Internal Affairs	Nei Wu Fu	内务府
Nine Dragon Screen	Jiu Long Bi	九龙壁
Northern Gate of Peace (Gate of Earthly Peace)	Bei An Men (Di An Men)	北安门（地安门）
Office for Administering Eunuchs	Jing Shi Fang	敬事房
Palace of Accumulated Purity	Zhong Cui Gong	锺粹宫
Palace of Celestial Favor	Cheng Qian Gong	承乾宫
Palace of Compassion and Tranquility	Ci Ning Gong	慈宁宫
Palace of Double Brilliance	Chong Hua Gong	重华宫
Palace of Earthly Tranquility	Kun Ning Gong	坤宁宫
Palace of Eternal Harmony	Yong He Gong	永和宫
Palace of Eternal Longevity	Yong Shou Gong	永寿宫
Palace of Eternal Spring	Chang Chun Gong	长春宫
Palace of Gathered Elegance	Chu Xiu Gong	储秀宫
Palace of Great Benevolence	Jing Ren Gong	景仁宫
Palace of Great Brilliance	Jing Yang Gong	景阳宫
Palace of Heavenly Purity	Qian Qing Gong	乾清宫
Palace of Prolonging Happiness	Yan Xi Gong	延禧宫
Palace of the Bringing-forth of Blessings	Yu Qing Gong	毓庆宫

English	Chinese Pinyin	Chinese
Palace of Tranquility and Longevity	Ning Shou Gong	宁寿宫
Palace of Universal Happiness	Xian Fu Gong	咸福宫
Palace of Upholding Earth	Yi Kun Gong	翊坤宫
Pavilion for Good Wishes	Fu Wang Ge	符望阁
Pavilion of Abundant View	Fu Lan Ting	富览亭
Pavilion of Appreciating Lush Scenery	Cui Shang Lou	萃赏楼
Pavilion of Assembling Fragrance	Ji Fang Ting	辑芳亭
Pavilion of Auspicious Clarity	Cheng Rui Ting	澄瑞亭
Pavilion of Brilliant Prospects	Li Jing Xuan	丽景轩
Pavilion of Ceremonial Purification	Xi Shang Ting	禊赏亭
Pavilion of Great Happiness	Jing Qi Ge	景祺阁
Pavilion of Green Ripples	Fu Bi Ting	浮碧亭
Pavilion of Literary Profundity	Wen Yuan Ge	文渊阁
Pavilion of Old Flowers	Gu Hua Xuan	古华轩
Pavilion of Panoramic View	Zhou Shang Ting	周赏亭
Pavilion of Pleasant Sounds	Chang Yin Ge	畅音阁
Pavilion of Prolonged Sunshine	Yan Hui Ge	延晖阁
Pavilion of Prolonging Spring	Yan Chun Ge	延春阁
Pavilion of Wonderful View	Guan Miao Ting	观妙亭
Right Gate of Chang An	Chang An You Men	长安右门
Right Gate of Peace	You An Men	右安门
Room for Diligent Retired Life	Juan Qin Zhai	倦勤斋
Room of Spiritual Cultivation	Yang Xing Zhai	养性斋
Room of Three Hopes (Room of Three Rarities)	San Xi Tang	三希堂
Room of Three Rarities (Room of Three Hopes)	San Xi Tang	三希堂
Scenic Hill (Jing Hill)	Jing Shan	景山
Sea Terrace Islet	Ying Tai	瀛台
Southern Study	Nan Shu Fang	南书房
Swan-goose Wing Tower (Five Phoenix Tower)	Yan Chi Lou (Wu Feng Lou)	雁翅楼（五凤楼）
Temple of Heaven	Tian Tan	天坛
Ten-thousand-spring Pavilion	Wan Chun Ting	万春亭
The First Gate of Heaven	Tian Yi Men	天一门
The Six Eastern Palaces	Dong Liu Gong	东六宫
The Six Western Palaces	Xi Liu Gong	西六宫
Thousand-autumn Pavilion	Qian Qiu Ting	千秋亭
Well of Concubine Zhen	Zhenfei Jing	珍妃井
Western Gate of Peace	Xi An Men	西安门
Western Prosperity Gate	Xi Hua Men	西华门
Western Swan-goose Wing Tower	Xi Yan Chi Lou	西雁翅楼
Western Warm Chamber	Xi Nuan Ge	西暖阁
Zhen Hill (Dominating Hill, Longevity Hill)	Zhen Shan (Wan Sui Shan)	镇山（万岁山）

Palace Rules and Human Order —From Gate of Heavenly Peace to Meridian Gate

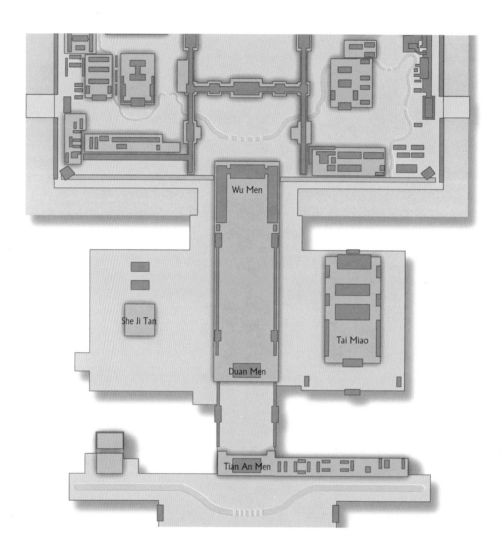

Plan of the Gate of Heavenly Peace to the Meridian Gate

Gate of Heavenly Peace: Symbol of Supremacy of Imperial Power

The map of the City of Beijing today is just like a chessboard dotted with checks big and small, and seated noticeably at the center of this chessboard pattern are the Gate of Heavenly Peace and the Palace Museum. The Gate of Heavenly Peace used to be the frontal gate of the dismantled Imperial City in the Ming and Qing Dynasties, and a major gateway to the Meridian Gate in the south.

The Gate of Heavenly Peace was first constructed in the 15th year of the Yongle Empire (1417), known then as Cheng Tian Men (the Heavenly Gate), and was reconstructed in the 8th year of Shunzhi Empire in the Qing Dynasty, renamed as the Gate of Heavenly Peace. Emperors in ancient times would denote themselves Tian Zi, meaning "son of Heaven." "Tian" in "Cheng Tian Men" (the Heavenly Gate) and "Tian An Men" (the Gate of Heavenly Peace) carries the same meaning: heaven. The implication being that "the emperor is one who is enlightened by and acts upon the will of Heaven." Upon this basis a

The Gate of Heavenly Peace (known as Gate of the Nation, a symbol of Beijing and as well as a symbol of China, twice reconstructed in 1952 and 1970)

further message of "unity and peace under Heaven" is added to the Gate of Heavenly Peace.

The magnificent Gate of Heavenly Peace that stands so proudly before the world today has, on the whole, retained its original appearance and shape after its renovation in the years of Shunzhi. The structure features a gate tower at the top with a unique design of double eave and gable-hip roof. The gate tower is nine bays wide from east to west and five bays deep from south to north. Nine in width and five in depth has a signification of 九五 (nine five), meaning "a flying dragon in the skies." According to the astrologers in ancient times, "nine" is the negative extreme and "five" the positive mean. The combination of the two symbolizes "emperor," signifying the supremacy of the throne. The so-called "flying dragon in the skies" is interpreted as an emperor flying like a dragon high up in the skies, after his ascendance to the throne.

Below the gate tower is a dark-red brick platform over ten meters in height. Under the platform is an exquisitely-carved white marble pedestal of Buddha's statue, which measures over 2000 square meters. The entire structure is 33.7 meters high. Its red walls, golden tiles, painted rafters, engraved beams and well-balanced shape have all contributed to an architectural structure, lofty and dignified, harmonious and majestic.

In 199 BC, Liu Bang came to the throne as the first emperor of the Han Dynasty. He was not happy at Prime Minister Xiao He's suggestion of large-scale construction to build the Wei Yang into a magnificent imperial palace. Xiao He replied, "Earth is where the Son of Heaven dwells. There can be no supremacy without the magnificence about the dwelling." This sentiment has well reflected the subtlety of the architecture of the imperial palace and its close relationship with the politics of an imperial power.

Just imagine how much of a shock it could arouse in one emotionally to look up at this colossal architectural complex of over thirty meters in height from an agricultural context!

There stands the magnificent gate tower in lovely and striking contrast with the insignificance of the humble subjects and the working people.

The blue and clear outer Golden Water River flows in front of the Gate of Heavenly Peace, with seven delicately-carved white marble bridges lying across the river. The easternmost bridge and the westernmost bridge are called Gong Sheng Qiao (Common Bridges), leading to the Laboring People's Cultural Palace (formerly the Imperial Ancestral Temple) and Zhongshan Park (formerly She Ji Tan, the Altar of Land and Grain) respectively. The other five are called Exterior Golden Water Bridges and directly face the five gateways. Two pairs of awe-inspiring and sincere stone lions are seated with two pairs of tall and straight ornamental columns erected below the gate tower (one pair behind the Gate of Heavenly Peace), which are so ingeniously proportioned and perfectly matched with one another, making the Gate of Heavenly Peace a complete architectural masterpiece of immense scope.

The Golden Water Bridges used to be heavily branded with a social estate system. Ordinarily, only the two Common Bridges were used when people are going in and out, instead of the Golden Water Bridges, which were open when the emperor was to pass through the Gate of Heavenly Peace. However, strict restrictions were set on the use of the Golden Water

Left: Ornamental Columns (in front of a palace or tomb, originated, according to legends, in ancient Yao and Shun years from a wood column that means they are always ready to accept good advice)

Bridges. The widest bridge in the middle with dragon patterns carved on the stone guardrails is called Yu Lu Qiao (the Bridge of Imperial Way), which was exclusively for use by the emperor. The two bridges on either side of the Bridge of Imperial Way were for the accompanying princes and dukes to cross, which are called Wang Gong Qiao (the Bridge for Royals). The following two are Pin Ji Qiao (High-rank Bridges), which were reserved for the officials and officers of the first to the third ranks in the Qing Dynasty. Likewise, the five gateways of the Gate of Heavenly Peace have their own rank distinctions. The largest in the middle is the imperial pathway reserved for the emperor. The smaller gateways on the east side and the west side of the imperial pathway were for princes, dukes and ministers to enter and exit. The two remaining small gateways are designed for use by the officials and officers of the fourth rank and below.

Normally, emperors did not enter or exit the Imperial Palace through the Gate of Heavenly Peace except for on special occasions such as a sacrificial ceremony at Tian Tan (the Temple of Heaven) on the Winter Solstice, "till the land" at Xian Nong Tan (the Altar of Agriculture) in spring, and a sacrificial ceremony at Di Tan (the Altar of the Earth) on the Summer Solstice. The mighty attending honor guard would then be split into five columns, marching out of the Gate of Heavenly Peace and crossing the seven stone bridges in reformed seven columns.

In the Ming and Qing Dynasties, the Gate of Heavenly Peace was the place where imperial edicts were most frequently issued. Imperial edicts were divided into two types: edicts announcing to the entire public the origin and date of the ascendance of a new emperor to the throne; and edicts announcing a title to be granted to an empress or a prince. When an imperial edict was scheduled, a platform would be set in front of the gate tower of the Gate of Heavenly Peace. A minister of the Ministry of Rites took over the imperial edict from the emperor at the Hall of Supreme Harmony and then ascended the Gate of Heavenly Peace. The officials and officers of various ranks as well as the "average people" dressed as if they are workmen, farmhands, merchants or students and soldiers stood as a mark of respect at the south of the Golden Water Bridges. When the ceremony started, those present all knelt down facing the gate tower, and this is the moment when the power and prestige of an emperor and the royalty and goodness of the subjects were incisively and vividly displayed through such performance.

Palace City, Imperial Palace, City of Beijing

The once solemn and mysterious Gate of Heavenly Peace is now open to the general public. Ascend to the top of the city gate tower and you will have a panoramic view of the beautiful city of Beijing.

Looking south, one sees the fascinating Tiananmen Square, which measures 440,000 square meters, ranking the largest of all city squares the world over.

Not far to the north of the gate tower is the lofty and majestic Imperial Palace, once the Palace City of the City of Beijing in the Ming and Qing Dynasties. Let's take a brief look at the origin of the Imperial Palace and the inter-relationships among the Palace City, the Imperial Palace and the City of Beijing.

Zhu Di, emperor of Ming, reverently called Ming Chengzu (founder of the Imperial Palace)

In 1399, Zhu Di, Prince of Yan and the fourth son of Emperor Zhu Yuanzhang, dispatched troops from Beiping on the pretext of exterminating traitors. His real intention, however, was to usurp the power from his nephew Emperor Jianwen. After taking the throne, Zhu Di, Emperor Yongle, renamed Beiping as Beijing, and moved the capital from Nanjing to Beijing.

In terms of urban development, this offered an unprecedented golden opportunity for Beijing.

Beijing was first formed as a capital city in the Liao Dynasty, which was called Nanjing (as a secondary capital), before being named Central Capital in the Jin Dynasty. It was not until in the Yuan Dynasty that Beijing was eventually set as its capital and given the name of Great Yuan Capital. Since then Beijing has experienced a rapid rise, growing in dimension to be the national political and commercial center. Marco Polo, Italian tourist and businessperson, spared no praise for the capital, acclaiming Great Yuan Capital to be the most magnificent and prosperous city unparalleled in the world at that time. In terms of the development of the Great Yuan Capital achieved thus far, Beijing in the Ming Dynasty became a pinnacle of construction and development in ancient China.

In the fourth year of Yongle (1406), Zhu Di, the then emperor, issued an imperial edict to construct an imperial palace at the former location of the imperial palace of the Yuan Dynasty. About two hundred and thirty thousand artisans, one million civilian laborers and a large number of soldiers were summoned for the construction, which lasted for 15 years and was finally completed in the 18th year of Yongle (1420).

Many contemporary historians have investigated the relationship between architecture and ancient civilization. They have all turned their eyes to the Pyramids in Egypt and the remains of the Inca Empire of Peru, the Great Wall of China ... Yet, Beijing and its Imperial Palace in the Ming and Qing Dynasties, too, deserve their attention. The corresponding civilization and wealth, the corresponding thoughts and religion, the corresponding social structure and development motivations might be hidden within Beijing and its Imperial Palace.

In the Yongle years of the Ming Dynasty, the planning of the urban area of Beijing was based mainly on the pattern of the Great Yuan Capital with necessary modifications. In the Ming Dynasty, like in the Yuan Dynasty, the Imperial City was built outside the Palace City. The Imperial City is located a little to the south of the center of the City of Beijing, surrounded with high walls with a gateway on each of the four sides. The north gateway was called Bei An Men (the Northern Gate of Peace, renamed Di An Men, the Gate of Earthly Peace in the Qing Dynasty), the east gateway Dong An Men (the Eastern Gate of Peace), the west gateway Xi An Men (the Western Gate of Peace), and the south gateway—the main gateway—the Heavenly Gate. Bei Hai, Zhong Hai, Nan Hai, Tai Miao (the Imperial Ancestral Temple) and the Altar of Land and Grain are all enclosed within the Imperial City. The Palace City is the core, encircled by the Imperial City, which is hemmed in by the City of Beijing. Within the area of the Imperial City there are roads

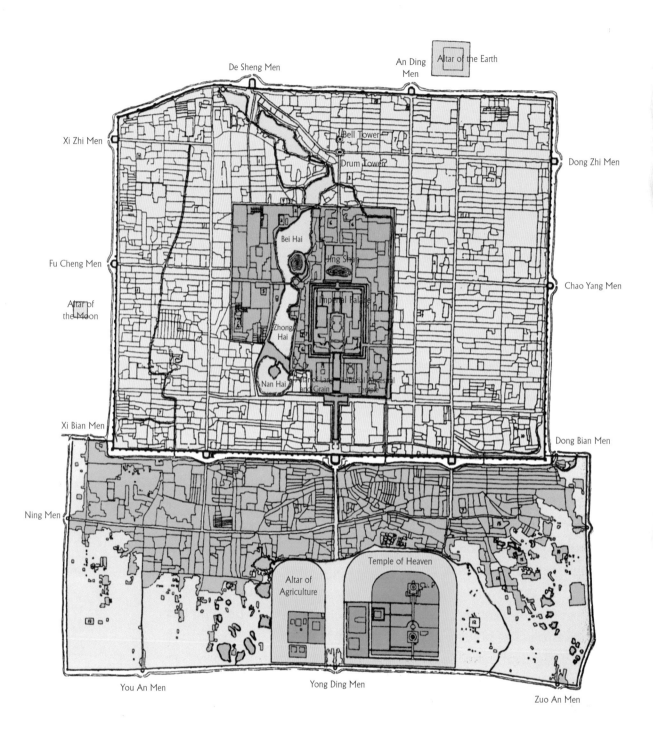

Palace City, Imperial Palace, Inner City and Outer City of Beijing in Ming and Qing Dynasties

for imperial carriages, villas for imperial families, temples, residences for high-ranking officials, and various facilities that serve the emperors and their families. It was not until the year 1553 that an outer city was added, and the former City of Beijing thus became the inner city.

A T-shaped court square is constructed in front of the Heavenly Gate, with palace walls on the east, west and south sides. There are gateways at the east wing, the west wing and the south end of this enclosed square. The east gateway is called Chang An Zuo Men (the Left Gate of Chang An), the west gateway Chang An You Men (the Right Gate of Chang An), and the south gateway Da Ming Men (the Great Ming Gate, changed into Da Qing Men, the Great Qing Gate in the Qing Dynasty and then into Gate of China—the Gate of China in the period of Republic of China, and then later removed). To the south of the Great Ming Gate is the main gate of the inner city of Beijing, which is called Zheng Yang Men (the Due South Gate) and what is known today as Qian Men (the Front Gate) at the south side of Tiananmen Square.

After a dynastic shift into the Qing Dynasty, the rulers continued to stay in the Palace City and the Imperial Palace, and expanded, renovated or renamed only a few places, such as the Great Ming Gate having been changed into the Great Qing Gate, and the Heavenly Gate into the Gate of Heavenly Peace. The overall layout of the City of Beijing remained essentially unchanged.

From the 20th century onwards, the City of Beijing has undergone tremendous changes. The walls of

Tiananmen Square

Prosperous Imperial Capital (a painting depicting a scene of commercial prosperity in Beijing from the last years of Emperor Jiajing to the early years of Emperor Wanli)

the T-shaped square have been dismantled and, instead, chang'an Avenue has been formed, and the Tiananmen Square of today has been planned and constructed.

The architecture and original styles and features of the Imperial Palace and its surrounding area have all been well preserved as they were in the Ming and Qing Dynasties.

"Ancestor's Temple on the Left, Altar of Land and Grain on the Right" and the Central Axis

According to the "Notes on Handicraft" in *Rites of Zhou*, an ancient classical work, the core principle in city planning is that the capital city should be square in form, with each side measuring nine *li* (Chinese unit of distance, equal to 500 meters) in length and three of the four sides should have three gateways each. In the city proper there should be nine straight streets crossed by nine transverse streets; ancestor's temple should be located on the left and alter of land and grain on the right; the front part (facing south) is devoted to the court, while the rear part (facing north) to business. This square-shaped design in city planning as highlighted in *Rites of Zhou* was accepted and handed down by the empires thereafter, and has been further developed in the actual practice of construction.

The Great Yuan Capital (today's Beijing) was composed of the Outer City, the Imperial Palace and the Palace City, providing a good example of the ancient principle and concept of "Ancestor's Temple on the Left, Altar of Land and Grain on the Right" and "Court at the Front and Marketplace at the Rear." Emperor Yongle of the Ming Dynasty decided to make Beijing the capital city, having the Imperial Ancestral Temple and the Altar of Land and Grain on two sides before the Palace City of the Imperial Palace. This has given great prominence to the arrangement of "Ancestor's Temple on the Left, Altar of Land and Grain on the Right." Later, the convenience provided by the waterway in the southeast part of the City of Beijing encouraged many business people to gather there and turning this area into its business center instead of its "rear marketplace" in the north of the Palace City of the Imperial City, thus breaking up the original pattern.

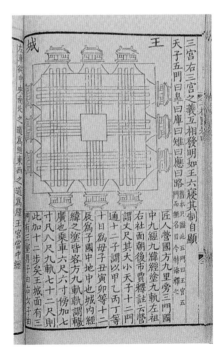

Plan of a Zhou Imperial City

The Ancestor's Temple (Ancestral Temple in the Ming and Qing Dynasties, and Beijing Laboring People's Cultural Palace since 1950)

Places for emperors to offer sacrifices to Heaven, Earth, the Sun and the Moon were constructed in the suburbs around the City of Beijing in the Ming Dynasty: the Temple of Heaven in the south, the Altar of the Earth in the north, the Altar of the Sun in the east, and the Altar of the Moon in the west. Then, the Altar of Agriculture was built to the west of the Temple of Heaven. The construction of an outer city was afterwards scheduled, and the two temples were enclosed within the Inner City, with the Altar of the Sun, the Altar of the Moon and the Altar of the Earth remaining in the Outer City.

The principal rule of keeping the central axial line running through the whole city was followed and highlighted throughout the entire planning of the City of Beijing in the Ming Dynasty; and this central axial line was superimposed upon that of the Imperial Palace. Liang Sicheng, a well-known contemporary architect, has fervently complimented, "This is the longest and the greatest central axial line from south to north the world has ever seen," and "The unique majestic and glorious order of Beijing is formed by this central axial line, [the city's] undulate shape to the front and to the rear, its balanced form on the right and on the left, and its spatial division is all based on this central axial line."

The central axial line starts northward from the main gateway of Yong Ding Men (the Gate of Eternal Settlement) of the Outer City (namely, along what is now the Inner Avenue of the Gate of Eternal Settlement and then to the Qianmen Avenue) with the Temple of Heaven and the Altar of Agriculture on the left and on the right; it then crosses the Due South Gate (now the Front Gate), the Great Ming Gate, and directly reaches the Heavenly Gate (now the Gate of Heavenly Peace) before entering the Imperial City and the Palace City, with the Imperial Ancestral Temple and the Altar of Land and Grain arranged on the left and on the right, and important halls upon the central axial line accompanied on either side by the imperial residences and halls. The line then goes through Jing Hill and the middle pavilion on the Hill and out from the Gate of Earthly Peace (known as the Back Gate) in the north of the Imperial City, and finally arrives at the Drum Tower and the Bell Tower in the northern end of the Inner City. Liang Sicheng says, "Upon its arrival at the Bell Tower, the central axial line has achieved a nice conclusion as planned. The line will no longer stretch out northward to reach the wall root, and instead divides evenly the pivot to the two city gates respectively on either side—An Ding Men (the Gate of Stability) and De Sheng Men (the Gate of Victory). There can be no overall architectural layout in this world so daring in terms of the arrangement of space in such a way."

A bird's-eye view of the Gate of Heavenly Peace and the Gate of Uprightness

Phoenixes Gathered in the Palace: A Sign of Auspiciousness

A walk northward from the Gate of Heavenly Peace and across Duan Men (the Gate of Uprightness) leads to the Meridian Square.

In ancient times, *zi* (子) meant "north" and *wu* (午) "south." The Meridian Gate is built along the north-south central axis of Beijing, seated at the center facing the sun. Hence the name the Meridian Gate (午门, or 午阙). The Gate of Uprightness is built outside the Meridian Gate. *Duan* (端) means "right" or "exactly," and *duan* and *wu*, when put together, means "directly to the sun." According to the science of Yin and Yang, the names of the Gate of Uprightness and the Meridian Gate imply the sense of expelling evils.

The two observation platforms on the left and the right ends of the tower terrace of the Meridian Gate protrude, forming a ⊓ shape from above. There are three gates at the front of the tower structure, with two unnoticeable side doors on either side, known as "five as if three." *Wu* (五, means "five") has the same pronunciation as noon in Chinese.

The Meridian Gate is a grand and majestic structure, and its terrace is one meter higher than the wall of the Imperial Palace. Upon the terrace, right in the center is the main city tower, about nine bays in width and three bays in depth. On both sides of the main tower are two corridors, extending southwards to the two towers on the protruding parts of the

Square at the Meridian Gate (where honor guard shows used to be performed and a punishment of flogging with a stick of officials executed)

Meridian Gate, which are named Yan Chi Lou (Swan-goose Wing Tower). A square-shaped pavilion stands around the corner of each of the two towers and at each of the southern ends. The four pavilions are all double eave, four ridges and pyramidal roof. The main tower, the pavilions, the corridors and the terrace form an architectural complex strewn at random, yet in perfect balance. The main tower and the four pavilions leave an impression of "five phoenixes gathering together, stretching out their wings, ready to fly." With this association, the tower is also known as the Five Phoenix Tower. The gathering of five phoenixes carries an auspicious message of luck and happiness.

The Meridian Gate was constructed in the 18th year of Yongle of the Ming Dynasty (1420), reconstructed in the 4th year of Shunzhi of the Qing Dynasty (1647), and renovated in the 6th year of Jiaqing of

The Meridian Gate (a view from the north)

the same Dynasty (1801). The Gate boasts an architectural floorage of 1,773.3 square meters, ranking the tallest of all the four city towers in the Imperial Palace. Among the architectural structures in the Imperial Palace, the Meridian Gate is next to the Hall of Supreme Harmony in total area, superior to the Gate of Heavenly Peace but a little inferior to the Hall of Supreme Harmony in height, an indication of its great scale and position.

"To be pushed out of the Meridian Gate and beheaded for public scorn," is a legend popular among people. Yet, this perception of the Meridian Gate as an execution ground is quite a misunderstanding. The Meridian Gate, aside from being an important routeway in and out of the Palace City, served mainly as a location for major ceremonial activities, for instance, upon grand ceremonies and important holidays, such as imperial enthronements, imperial weddings, empress entitlements, memorial ceremonies, New Year's Day (present-day Spring Festival), midwinter's day, and the emperor's birthday; a guard of honor—a symbol of imperial power and dignity—was displayed at the Meridian Gate.

On a triumphant return of the army, the emperor would personally ascend the Meridian Gate to conduct the ceremony of "taking over the captives," on the occasion of which the captives will be presented by the officers and soldiers to the emperor.

The ritual of the annual announcement of the almanac was also held here. On the first day of the 12th month of the lunar year, the almanac of the coming year was made public at the Meridian Gate.

In addition, a bell and a drum are fixed upon the city tower, which were sounded simultaneously on important occasions. The toll of the bell and the beating of the drum could be heard as far away as ten miles off.

Purple Palace: Link between Heaven and Earth

Before touring the Forbidden City, we should ask ourselves one question—what does "the Forbidden City" mean exactly?

Before it acquired this name, the Forbidden City was commonly called the Purple Palace. "Purple," in this context, does not refer to a color that is created by mixing blue and red together, but rather to a heavenly concept. In ancient times, the color purple was closely associated with a constellation called Purple Palace. Astronomers at that time used to divide the fixed stars in the celestial body into three colonies. The mid colony consists of fifteen stars, with Polaris being the center, which is also known as Zi Yuan or Zi Wei (purple star). Purple Palace was believed to be the Heavenly Palace, home of God of Heaven. Since the emperor would self-style himself as the Son of Heaven, it was only natural that the configuration and movement of the stars were accepted as a concept applicable to the human world, and this accounts for the naming of the Imperial Palace as Purple Palace.

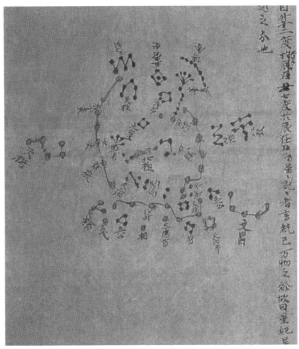

A map of Polaris in *Zhan Yun Qi Shu* (a scientific work in the late Tang Dynasty and the Five Dynasties. The Chinese have long been known to associate astronomical phenomena with human affairs)

Whatever the name, the Heavenly Palace or Imperial Palace was a heavily guarded place forbidden to common people, and hence the name Forbidden City.

Legend says that the Forbidden City used to have 9999.5 rooms. You might wonder how there could be a half room. It is most likely related to the Heavenly Palace, which, according to legend, has ten thousand rooms. As the emperors on earth would not dare to compare their own palace with the Heavenly Palace, they deducted half a room from their own inferior palace. So there is a half room, which is said to be the small room on the west side under Wen Yuan Ge (the Pavilion of Literary Profundity).

While there were originally more than 9000 houses in the Forbidden

Corner Tower (built at the four corners of the enclosed city wall, elegant and magnificent; the building is constructed of nine beams, eighteen pillars, tri-eaves and seventy-two ridges)

City in the Qing Dynasty, this figure had dropped to 8662 by the year 1955, resulting from human or natural factors in the long passage of eventful years.

A city wall 3,428 meters in length encloses the Forbidden City. The average thickness of the wall is 7.5 meters, with rammed earth stuffed in between the brick-laid surfaces. The city moat outside the wall is six-meter-deep Tongzi River. The Forbidden City is so strongly fortified with severe palace prohibitions that it well deserves its name.

The walls of most of the architectural structures within the Forbidden City are red and the tiles yellow. The colors are strikingly glaring and sumptuous. According to the theory of the five elements in ancient times, yellow represents "earth," and "center" as well as signifying "nobleness." Since the Sui and Tang Dynasties, the color yellow had gradually grown to be a color exclusively for use by emperors. The common people were not allowed to apply this color arbitrarily, or they would be accused of acting against the norms of etiquette. It was not until the Ming and Qing Dynasties that rules were formulated, specifying that yellow-glazed tiles were only for use on structures such as imperial palaces, imperial mausoleums, and temples as built upon an imperial edict.

The color red symbolizes rejoicing, satisfaction, happiness, dignity and elegance, flaring and refined. Commencing from the Zhou Dynasty, red became widely applied in palace architecture, and this tradition has been handed down generation after generation ever since.

The use of red and yellow for the two base colors for the Forbidden City, displays the noble qualities of China and the imperial spirit of an empire in the

Decorative door nails for the Meridian Gate (applied to many doors in the Forbidden City, arranged in nine rows or lines with nine nails in each, another example of number worship)

midst of dignity and solemnity. In violent contrast with the base colors of gray, black and white as adopted in the residences in the City of Beijing, the red walls and yellow tiles exhibit a sacredness and inviolability.

There are still another three city gates beyond the Meridian Gate—the Gate of Divine Prowess in the north, Dong Hua Men (the Eastern Prosperity Gate) in the east and Xi Hua Men (the Western Prosperity Gate) in the

The Eastern Prosperity Gate

The Western Prosperity Gate (The Eastern Prosperity Gate is for officials to enter the court and the Western Prosperity Gate to exit from the court. The Eastern Prosperity Gate is also the resting place for the deceased emperor, hence the name of Ghost Gate.)

west. The Eastern Prosperity Gate and the Western Prosperity Gate are set close to the south end on either side of their respective city walls, instead of the middle section of the east and the west city walls. The reason is not difficult to determine: The Meridian Gate as the main south gate is of a special importance, and there are rules restricting the entry into and exit from this gate. For need of officials for errands in the court and various other considerations, the Eastern Prosperity Gate and the Western Prosperity Gate would be opened at the two sides not far away from the Meridian Gate as a compensation for the inconvenience thus caused.

Wielding of Supreme Imperial Power on the Will of Heaven

—Three Grand Halls

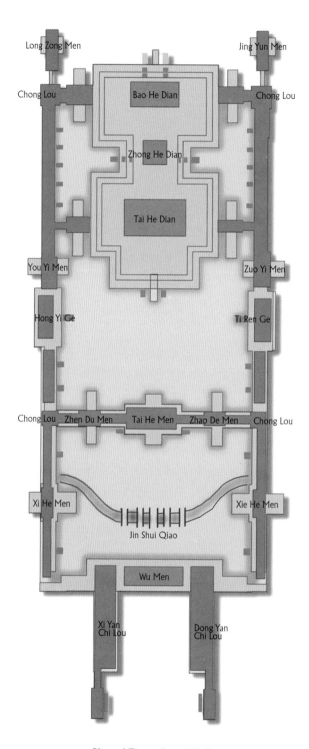

Long Zong Men

Jing Yun Men

Chong Lou

Bao He Dian

Chong Lou

Zhong He Dian

Tai He Dian

You Yi Men

Zuo Yi Men

Hong Yi Ge

Ti Ren Ge

Chong Lou   Zhen Du Men   Tai He Men   Zhao De Men   Chong Lou

Xi He Men

Xie He Men

Jin Shui Qiao

Wu Men

Xi Yan
Chi Lou

Dong Yan
Chi Lou

Plan of Three Grand Halls

Gate of Supreme Harmony and the Three Grand Halls

Walk through the Meridian Gate and you will see the Gate of Supreme Harmony, the tallest and biggest palatial gate of the existing ancient architectural structures in China. In the early Ming Dynasty the Gate of Supreme Harmony was called Feng Tian Men (the Gate of Offering Heaven), renamed the Gate of Great Supremacy in the years of Jiajing, and has been called the Gate of Supreme Harmony since the reign of Shunzhi of the Qing Dynasty.

Between the Meridian Gate and the Gate of Supreme Harmony lies the largest square in the Imperial Palace at around 30,000 square meters. The Jade Belt River winds across the square and five stone bridges span the river. Here, greatness and magnificence merge perfectly into one organic unit.

The Gate of Supreme Harmony is the main gate to the Frontal Three Halls: the Hall of Supreme Harmony, the Hall of Central Harmony and the Hall of Preserving Harmony. The halls are seated upon a three-meter-high Xumi base. Xumi, according to

Square at the Gate of Supreme Harmony (a gray-white stone-paved imperial road in the middle that runs throughout the Forbidden City and forms the central axis of the City of Beijing)

The Gate of Supreme Harmony (where many important ceremonies were held, and emperors used to enter and exit.)

the Buddhist legend, is a holy mountain, said by some to be the Himalayas. Xumi is believed to be the pedestal of Buddha's statue, and Xumi is used for the base of the three halls to give prominence to and sing praises of the imperial power with the aid of the greatness of Buddhism. The use of this architectural style is not uncommon in China from the Sui and Tang Dynasties onwards.

The Gate of Supreme Harmony is 23.8 meters high and nine bays wide with three gates. Two big copper lions with open mouths and glaring eyes are assigned on the right and left of the gate, guarding the entrance. In those days emperors of the Ming Dynasty would come here to personally conduct the state affairs. Before dawn, courtiers—officials and officers— hurried over here to the morning court while the sovereign sat upright in his seat, receiving the respects and holding the court.

Three Grand Halls (the most important architectural complex in the Imperial Palace, which is where the soul of the Ming and Qing empires lies)

The Three Grand Halls are built on a very large terrace base of 232 meters long from south to north and 130 meters wide from east to west. This 工-shaped white-marble terrace base is composed of three flights of stairs, which measure over 8 meters in height and 25,000 square meters in total area. Stone railings fence the three flights of stairs, with balusters erected every one meter along the railings. There are 1458 balusters in all, each carved with either a dragon or a phoenix pattern. Under these balusters are 1,142 intricately-carved stone dragon heads, which are also called *chishou* (*chi*, a kind of hornless dragon in Chinese ancient legend, *shou* means "head"). These stone dragon heads with their staring eyes and open mouths add a bold and vigorous brush stroke to the forbidden place of great importance and exhibit a fine piece of work where art and practicality are cleverly combined.

The white-marble terrace base of the Three Grand Halls

The mouth of each stone dragon head actually serves as a passageway for the drainage of rainwater. On wet days, rain comes down through the 1142 narrow passages from one flight of stairs down to the one below, before merging into the underground drain. Even during the heaviest of downpours, the rainwater will instantly be drained clear, with hundreds of white water columns swarming out of the dragons' mouths and drumming the ground with deafening crashes. If you happen to be here during heavy rain, you are sure to see a majestic scene that will become an unforgettable memory—one can't help but feel intoxicated in the midst of the symphony of heaven and earth.

Sundial

Copper tortoise

The spacious, heavy and resplendent Xumi bases prop up the Three Grand Halls, creating a unique stately and splendid image of great momentum. The Three Grand Halls deserve, in every sense, the title of the Center of the Imperial Palace, which forms the center of the entire City of Beijing.

The Three Grand Halls were initially constructed in the 18th year of the Yongle Empire (1420), which were then named Feng Tian Dian (the Hall of Offering Heaven), Hua Gai Dian (the Hall of Canopy), and Jin Shen Dian (the Hall of Practising Moral Culture), and renamed as Huang Ji Dian (the Hall of Imperial Supremacy, Zhong Ji Dian (the Hall of Central Supremacy), and Jian Ji Dian (the Hall of Administering Supremacy), before acquiring the present names in the second year of Shunzhi of the Qing Dynasty (1645). Supreme Harmony, Central Harmony and Preserving Harmony were originally quoted from Confucian literary works. According to *The Book of Changes*, *da* (大, big or great), namely *tai* (太), means the meeting of Yin and Yang (Yin: female or negative; Yang: male or positive), stimulating and enhancing

Jialiang

Copper crane

(Copper tortoise, coper crane, sundial and *jialiang* on the vermilion steps of stone leading up to the Hall of Supereme Harmony are symbols of power and eternity.)

Yuan Qi (Primordial Qi; essence), and hence bringing harmony to all on earth throughout the four seasons of spring, summer, autumn and winter. *The Book of Changes* says that if such harmony is achieved, everything on earth is on the right track. Qing people adopted Tai He (Supreme Harmony) to imply that the emperor acts upon the instructions of Heaven, enjoying supreme authority over his subordinates, who must comply, and, in the meantime, to express a wish for a satisfactory political and social order.

Zhong He (Central Harmony) is concerned with the golden mean as advocated by Confucians, originated from *The Doctrine of the Mean*, which says, "Where Zhong He is achieved, everything under the sun is in order, everything in life is satisfactory, and everyone on earth achieves what he desires and everything looks fresh and gay." Emperors tried to advertise themselves as faithfully abiding by Zhong He so as to show that they were just and restrained in their administration of the state affairs.

Confucianism attaches the greatest importance to *he* (和, peace), and Bao He (Preserving Harmony) may be interpreted as preserving and maintaining peace. And, in a more general sense, Bao He can mean the maintenance of harmony between heaven and earth and the coordination of relations of various natures.

The naming of an architectural structure in the Imperial Palace invariably contains a profound implication, well worth appreciating.

Supreme "Hall of Golden Throne"

Of the three grand halls, the one standing to the south is the Hall of Supreme Harmony, popularly reputed as the Hall of the Golden Throne. This is where emperors ascended to the throne and empresses crowned, birthdays celebrated, respects paid, and banquets offered; hence acquiring fame as the First Hall of China. No effort has been spared in making the hall so intricately designed and accomplished, it is therefore no wonder that it stands out so gloriously from all the others.

The present Hall of Supreme Harmony is a wooden structured masterpiece, which was reconstructed in the 36th year of the reign of

Small animals on the eaves of the Hall of Supreme Harmony (Odd number of small animals is normally adopted in the roof ornaments of a building in ancient China, such as 1, 3, 5, 7, and 9, the maximum being 9. But the number of ornamental animals applied to the Hall of Supreme Harmony is 10, so as to indicate its supremacy.)

Kangxi. It is 11 bays in width or about 64 meters; five bays in depth or 37 meters; and 35.05 meters in height; with a total architectural floorage measuring 2,377 square meters. Among the existing ancient buildings in China today, the Hall of Supreme Harmony ranks the top in size, depth and height.

The Hall of Supreme Harmony is characterized by its double eave and hip roof, a style that displays dignity. The roof ornaments are deliberately selected. Both ends of the main ridge are decorated with dragon-head-patterned volutes (building components of ornamental effect), each consisting of 13 pieces of glazed parts. The two big decorative objects are approximately 3.4 meters in height, 2.68 meters in width, and 2,125 kilograms in weight, well deserving of the prestigious title of No. 1 decorative parts of ancient buildings of China. Ten small animals are carved at the eave corners, which are quite exceptional. These animals are arranged in the following order: dragon, phoenix, lion, heavenly steed, sea horse,

Interior of the Hall of Supreme Harmony

Caisson ceiling painted in gold with a pattern of a dragon with a pearl in the mouth

suanni (a legendary lion), tooth fish, *xiezhi* (a mythical animal), corrida, and *xingshi*. *Xingshi* is a divine animal, which is seen only in the Hall of Supreme Harmony and which is a rare case in ancient architecture.

The Hall of Supreme Harmony is quite spacious. 72 enormous wooden columns are erected inside to hold the hall together. Of these columns, six in the central part of the hall are painted gold, and the rest purple-red. The caisson ceiling on the roof of the hall is painted in golden color a pattern of a dragon with a pearl in the mouth. The roof is round at the top and square in the lower part, 1.8 meters high, with a compartment ceiling 6 meters in diameter. The workmanship is delicate and the caisson ceiling is excellent in terms of ancient architecture. The caisson ceiling is not only of a decorative effect, but functions as a "stabilizer," which is regarded as an auspicious object. A golden-painted dragon chair and a dragon-carved screen are placed on the high wooden platform (a style of pedestal of Buddha's statue, also known as Golden Platform). In those days, the emperors sat in this chair, issuing commands in this glittering golden world.

Interior of the Hall of Supreme Harmony

The furnishings on either side of the dragon throne, such as an elephant, a *luduan* (mythological beast), a crane and a fragrance stand, are symbols of auspiciousness. The huge, softhearted elephant gives one a sense of sureness and tranquility and was often said to signify the stability of rule and the tranquility of society. An elephant with a vase (*ping*, homophonic to "peace" in Chinese) carried on his back symbolizes harvest and peace under the heaven. According to legend, the elephant is a multi-lingual divine animal, and it is a symbol of peace on earth when an elephant approaches carrying a treasure vase on his back. On either side of the imperial throne stands an enameled copper elephant.

The *luduan* is a legendary divine animal, which is able to speak different languages and walk a thousand miles a day. A pair of *luduan* set on either side of the throne foretells the coming of pilgrims from various directions. The crane is a symbol of long life and may also signify an eternal existence of the nation. A fragrance stand is a holder in which fragrant incense is burnt. It is said to represent peace and stability.

A general view of the Hall of Preserving Harmony (the harmony of the outer appearance and its implication, as well as the combination of the lines of the architecture worth noticing)

The Hall of Central Harmony and Its Various Roof Designs

To the north of the Hall of Supreme Harmony are the Hall of Central Harmony and the Hall of Preserving Harmony. First, let's take a close look at the Hall of Central Harmony.

Of the Three Grand Halls, the Hall of Central Harmony is the smallest in size, just over 580 square meters in area, with five bays both in length and in width. The shape of the Hall of Central Harmony is similar to a square pavilion, and the big fine-gold pearl right in the middle of the rooftop is truly impressive.

Before proceeding to a grand ceremony at the Hall of Supreme Harmony, emperors in those days would stop over here for a brief rest till things were all arranged and in order there. In this sense, the Hall of Central Harmony functioned more like a recess room along the way. Though, some ceremonies were also held here in this hall, such as the sacrificial rite at the Altar of Agriculture. Prior to the ceremony,

A general view of the Hall of Central Harmony

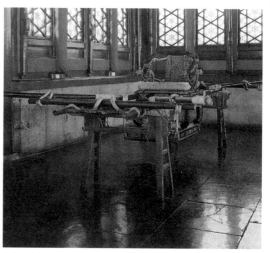

Interior of the Hall of Central Harmony (not as splendid as the Hall of Supreme Harmony, yet as refined and poised, acquiring the same elegant and resplendent quality)

Sedan chair

emperors would read the prayers and inspect the farm tools.

As in the Hall of Supreme Harmony and the Hall of Preserving Harmony, there is a throne placed in the Hall of Central Harmony, which is specifically arranged along the central axis of the City of Beijing to mark the supremacy of the emperor. The furnishings are relatively simple: a screen, a pair of elephant sculptures, a pair of *luduan*, a pair of fragrance stands and two pairs of tripods. The Hall is spacious, and is accessible from the doors on all four sides. A pair of charcoal braziers is therefore, placed to heat the hall in cold winters. Today, sedan chairs can be seen on the right and the left of the Hall, which were formerly used in the palace by emperors.

The Hall of Central Harmony features a four-corner pyramidal roof. The Hall is erected in between the Hall of Supreme Harmony's style of a double eave and hip roof and the Hall of Preserving Harmony's style of a double eave and gable-hip roof. Other styles of roofs are also noticed in the surrounding buildings, including single eave and hip roof, single eave and gable-hip roof, and flush gable roof, which help to distinguish between

Double eave and hip roof

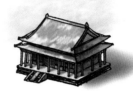

Double eave and gable-hip roof

Overhanging gable roof

Flush gable roof

Four-corner pyramidal roof

Palace roofs

Palace roofs

The roofs vary in ranking, in accordance with the following order: double eave and hip roof (like those of the Hall of Supreme Harmony and the Meridian Gate), double eave and gable-hip roof (like those of the Gate of Heavenly Peace and the Gate of Supreme Harmony), single eave and hip roof, single eave and gable-hip roof, overhanging gable roof, flush gable roof, four-corner pyramidal roof, and round ridge roof. The flush gable roof features a diagonal ridge for hip roof with two sloping sides. The pyramidal roof is generally applied to a square-shaped structure, which may be divided into the four-corner pyramidal roof and the round pavilion roof, the latter having no ridge.

the primary and the secondary; displaying a changing architectural style— vividness and diversity amongst strictness and unity.

Enormous roofs and high flights of stairs are major characteristics of China's ancient architecture. The former signifies heaven and the latter earth, with humans in between, constituting a concrete image and an underlying implication of the unity of "heaven, earth and man." Large roofs have remained much favored until the 20th century.

The Hall of Preserving Harmony and Imperial Examinations

The idea of minimizing the number of columns in the construction of the Hall of Preserving Harmony was adopted, resulting in a brighter and more spacious hall.

In the Ming Dynasty, emperors used to change their ceremonial robes here before and after a grand ceremony in the Hall of Supreme Harmony. Emperors of the Ming and Qing Dynasties liked to give banquets here. But what most deserves mention is that, by the end of the 16th century, the Hall of Preserving Harmony had become a location for the final imperial examination—the highest form of the imperial examinations in China.

The imperial examination system in the Ming and Qing Dynasties was deeply involved in formalism, and was greatly impaired by the prevalence of what is called the Eight-part Essay, a stereotyped writing. However, the examination procedure, on the other hand, turned out to be more and more strict and accomplished. Imperial Examinations included rural-level examinations, provincial-level examinations, metropolitan-level examinations and final court examinations. The examinee must pass the county-level and town-level examinations before being entered for a rural-level examination. The successful examinees of a rural-level examination were called Shengyuan or Xiucai. The provincial-level examination was held once every three years and was presided over by the Chief Supervisor

Interior of the Hall of Preserving Harmony (Gongshi were examined by the emperor in person in the Ming and Qing Dynasties, and exam questions were compiled and published by an imperial order. Despite a strict confidentiality system adopted then, cheating in a court examination was unavoidable.)

as authorized by the emperor. The successful examinees at the provincial-level examination were called Juren, of whom the number one was Xieyuan. The metropolitan examination took place in the capital, also once every three years, and was supervised by the Ministry of Rites. Juren from various provinces qualified for the metropolitan examination, and the successful examinees were called Gongshi, of whom the number one is entitled to the title of Huiyuan. Xiucai, Juren and Gongshi are not officials. Only those who have passed court examination are granted titles of officials by the imperial court. The court examination was the occasion for the selection of officials, and the examination took place in the palace and was supervised

Jinshi Admission Billboard

by the emperor himself. This is an indication that the imperial examinations were very highly respected in those years, and a court examination offers a golden opportunity for the emperor to show his benevolence.

The court examination presided over by the emperor is also called the palace examination. Grades of three ranks are granted to successful candidates. The first grade *Jinshi Jidi* is conferred to three Jinshi, of whom the number one was Zhuangyuan, the second winner Bangyan, and the third Tanhua; the second and the third grades to several candidates of Jinshi family background, or an equivalent-to-Jinshi family background.

The results of the court examination were unveiled at the Hall of Supreme Harmony. The examinees waited at the Gate of Heavenly Peace to be summoned. The newly-selected Jinshi would then enter the palace to be received by and to pay their respects to the emperor. This formality is called 传胪 (*chuanlu*). Thereafter, public notices were posted along the Chang'an Street for three days, announcing the names of the successful candidates. Golden-colored paper was used for the notice known as *jinbang* (golden billboard). To have one's name on a golden billboard was a long-cherished dream among scholars, and was regarded by Chinese as the greatest fortune ever experienced in one's life. This greatest happiness was once closely linked with the Hall of Preserving Harmony.

In the spring of 1904, history witnessed the final round of the imperial examinations in China, which was held in the Hall of Preserving Harmony. That year a serious drought occurred and spring sowing was difficult. It so happened that one of the examinees at the court examination was called Liu Chunlin, which was associated in implication with spring rain that dissolved the drought. Emperor Guangxu and Empress Dowager Cixi noticed the name, and believing the name to be an auspicious sign, Liu Chunlin was selected as the number one.

The original appearance of the Hall of Preserving Harmony has on the whole been well preserved, and is today as it was in the Qing Dynasty. The imperial throne, in which emperors used to sit when presiding over a court examination is still there, yet is devoid of the usual furnishings around it. Tables and chairs for an examination or a banquet were organized in place as occasion required.

The Son of Heaven and His Dragon World

Today, the dragon is the most well-known divine animal and symbol of

auspiciousness in China. This mascot in ancient times, however, was invariably exclusive to the emperors.

The emperor was worshipped as the Son of Heaven and everything about him was likely to be linked with the dragon, from his physical appearance down to his manner of talking and walking, and even his style of writing and residence The emperor was said to bear a dragon-like face, he slept in a dragon bed, wore a dragon robe, and sat in a dragon chair. The rise of a new emperor was described

The golden throne in the Hall of Supreme Harmony (The chair known as the nine-dragon throne is a legacy handed down from the Ming Dynasty to the Qing Dynasty, which symbolizes supreme imperial power. Yuan Shikai once replaced the throne with a sofa after he took over power.)

as the flying of a dragon, the offspring an emperor procreated was called "dragon's son," "dragon's grandson" or "dragon's breed," and the manner an emperor displayed was named "dragon's dignity." As a result, the Three Grand Halls, and, indeed, the entire Imperial Palace, were formed into a dragon world.

Around each of the six golden columns of the Hall of Supreme Harmony is painted a giant dragon twining upward with its head directly facing the top of the column with its mouth wide open, as if the dragon is riding on the clouds, braving the flying winds and surging waves. These dragons provide a glorious and magnificent sight.

A gold-painted throne with hollowed-out dragon patterns, handed down from the Ming Dynasty, is placed in the Hall of Supreme Harmony. Cloud-and-dragon patterns are carved on the back of the throne, and there are dragon patterns all over the chair, making the throne a real "dragon chair."

Left: Cloud-and-dragon step stone

Columns around the base of the Gate of Supreme Harmony are all carved with dragon and cloud patterns.

Gold crown of Emperor Wanli

Phoenix crown of Wanli's Empress Xiaoduan (ornamented with six golden dragon patterns and three phoenix patterns, constituting an auspicious dragon-phoenix design)

Behind the dragon chair stands a screen with patterns of flying dragons, and in front of it a pair of fragrance stands with five-claw dragon patterns. The coffered ceiling in the middle of the roof is also dragon-patterned, functioning as both an ornament and an auspicious object that dispels evils.

The cloud-and-dragon step stone has played a special role in this dragon world of the Three Grand Halls, which are located along the imperial road in the north of the Hall of Preserving Harmony. This is the biggest stone carving in the Palace, 16 meters long, 3 meters wide, 1.7 meters thick, and an estimated 250 tons in weight. The cloud-and-dragon pattern of nine dragons mounting the white clouds has attracted many tourists here. The overall picture looks vivacious, coherent and lifelike. The sea waves and cliffs against a setting of blue sky and white clouds at the bottom add to the magnificence to the entire carving.

These pictures, carvings and ornaments emphasize the glory of the dragon, the glory of the emperor, and the glory of imperial power.

Flying Dragon and Dancing Phoenix, Eventful Universe
—A Tour around the Three Rear Palaces

The Gate of Heavenly Purity (The Gate is a building-type gate with single eave and gable-hip roof; the square in front of the Gate functions as an important link between the court and the dwelling quarters.)

Space Conversion at the Gate of Heavenly Purity

To the north of the Hall of Preserving Harmony, a sidelong street 50 meters wide from south to north and 200 meters long from east to west draws clearly a dividing line between the Outer Palace and the Inner Court of the Forbidden City. Since the street goes right across in front of Qian Qing Men (the Gate of Heavenly Purity), people call it the Gate of Heavenly Purity Square.

Aside from the Gate of Heavenly Purity, the Square has Jing Yun Men (the Gate of Great Fortune in the east, the Long Zong Men (the Gate of Glorifying Forebears) in the west, the Left Back Gate and the Right Back Gate on the two sides of the Hall of Preserving Harmony in the south and the Left Inner Gate and the Right Inner Gate on the two sides of the Gate of Heavenly Purity in the north. The two interior gates are important entrances and the security measures there were particularly strict and severe.

As the Gate of Heavenly Purity used to be the front gate to the Inner Court in the Ming Dynasty, the Gate of Heavenly Purity Square actually performed the function of space conversion in that the Square marks the end of the architectural structures of the Outer Palace and the start of the architectural structures of the Inner Court. In addition, the Square makes it possible for the Three Front Halls and the Three Rear Palaces to link up, which used to be separated. The specially-designed narrow square added to the shortening of the distance between the Outer Palace and the Inner Court, making it easier for the emperor to attend court. The distance across the porches of the Hall of Preserving Harmony and the Gate of Heavenly

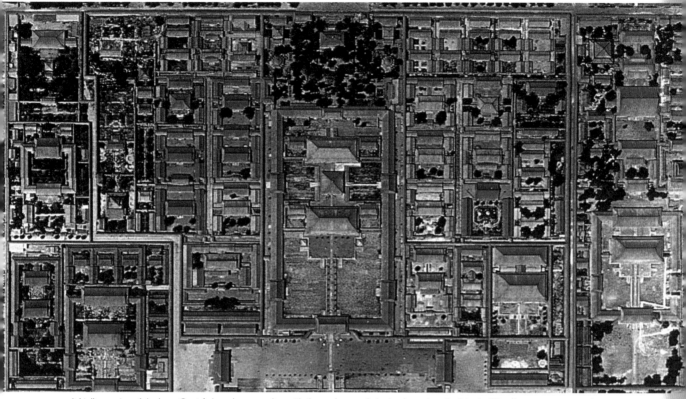

A bird's-eye view of the Inner Court (a legendary rear palace with three palaces and six chambers where lived, in the Ming Dynasty, as many as nine thousand concubines and imperial maids)

Purity is the narrowest section—about 30 meters in width.

State affairs in the Ming Dynasty were almost always discussed and attended to in the Three Grand Halls, whereas these activities in the Qing Dynasty were normally carried out further towards the residential quarters in the rear; and audiences with ministers were performed at the Gate of Heavenly Purity instead of the Gate of Supreme Harmony.

Emperor Kangxi was well known for being highly zealous and earnest. From the age of 16, he would go to the imperial court to administer state affairs—only failing to do so when he was not at the Imperial Palace— thus, he visited the court almost everyday from 7 o'clock or a little later in the morning for over 50 years. Prior to the arrival of Emperor Kangxi, the ministers were supposed to gather at either the Meridian

Gate before entering the Gate of Glorifying Forebears or the Gate of Great Fortune to await their own turns to present their respective memorandums to the emperor.

Emperors in the Qing Dynasty would often arrange some major conferences or receptions at the Gate of Heavenly Purity, and occasionally, title-awarding ceremonies for Jinshi. Wedding ceremonies for the crown

Auspicious jars (Big copper jars set along the two sides of the Gate of Heavenly Purity for fire fighting purposes, which are regarded as auspicious vessels)

prince or the princess were also held there, accounting for the increases in status of the Gate of Heavenly Purity over time. Some important authorities such as Privy Council (a military-political affair) were formed around the Gate of Heavenly Purity, which contributed much more to the function of the Gate of Heavenly Purity Square.

Emperor's Home: Flying Dragon and Dancing Phoenix

The Three Rear Palaces were first heard of in the mid-Ming Dynasty.

Earlier, only the Palace of Heavenly Purity and the Palace of Earthly Tranquility were known. During the years of Jiajing, the emperor, a palace called the Hall of Union was added in between the two palaces, thus making the Three Front Halls corresponding to the Three Rear Palaces. Similar to the Three Front Halls, the Three Rear Palaces were seated upon a ⼯-shaped white marble base. Though they may seem much smaller as residential architectural structures at the rear, they add more to the sense of home.

Golden dragons, golden phoenixes and colored royal seals were painted on some of the beams and wood stakes at the three rear palaces. Emperor Kangxi once wrote in "Ode to Zhao Ren Dian (the Hall of Manifest Mercy)," "On the girders and ridge beams are painted dancing phoenixes and flying dragons." It is only natural that the phoenix as a symbol of empress should dance with the emperor at this emperor's home, weaving a nest of dragon and phoenix.

The Hall of Union (a single eave and pyramidal roof architectural structure)

Like the Three Grand Halls, the Three Rear Palaces are surrounded with a long linked corridor, which forms an enclosed compound, with smaller complexes contained within larger ones. The Three Rear Palaces are composed of nine compounds, each palace consisting of its own three complexes. The palaces are arranged in three rows strictly according to the format of "one compound properly coupled with

Copper lion statues in front of the Gate of Heavenly Purity (two lions, each on either side of the home, with little sideways heads, looking toward the imperial)

two wing compounds." The compound of the Palace of Heavenly Purity stands in the front row, with the Hall of Manifest Mercy and Hong De Dian (the Hall of Primoting Virtue) as accompanying halls on either side of it. The two halls have individual compounds of their own. The compound of the Palace of Earthly Tranquility is positioned in the middle row, with Dong Nuan Ge (the Eastern Warm Chamber) and Xi Nuan Ge (the Western Warm Chamber) compounds on either side. In the back row is a compound formed of Kun Ning Men (the Gate of Earthly Tranquility), with the east compound of the Gate of Earthly Tranquility and the west compound of the Gate of Earthly Tranquility situated at its right side and left side.

The nine compounds are planned in parallel along the central axial line of the City of Beijing, reaching out with great momentum in a natural and harmonious manner in the northern part of the Three Grand Halls. In comparison, the height of the architecture is reduced and the density increased. A uniqueness as desired by dwelling quarters is displayed in the overall design. In those years, pot plants would be placed there in the compounds throughout the four seasons of the year. Finely-trimmed bamboo groves, tall and straight, would sway in the gentle wind, filled with vitality, comfort and warmth that a "home" is to offer, thus making themselves different from the front three halls in that there are no trees in the latter.

Emperors in the Qing Dynasty liked to give some major banquets at their own home, and the Palace of Heavenly Purity was normally the preferred location. Banquets were varied in name, such as New Year's Eve Banquet, Victory Banquet, Triumph Banquet, Classic Banquet, Birthday Banquet, Long Life Banquet, Emperor's Wedding Banquet, Princess's Wedding Feast, Book Compilation Banquet, Provincial Imperial Examination Banquet, Gratitude Banquet, etc. In the Qing Dynasty, this imperial home also experienced two grand Thousand Aged Banquet occasions, expressing a wish for peace and prosperity of the entire country as well as for long life for all people. One of these Thousand Ages Banquets took place in the 61st year of Emperor Kangxi, with an attendance of around one thousand people, and the other took place in the 50th year of Emperor Qianlong, with an attendance of over three thousand guests. It is not difficult to picture the magnificent festival and the jubilant atmosphere these banquets evoked.

The Palace of Heavenly Purity has housed 12 emperors in all, of whom 10 were Ming emperors, plus Shunzhi and Kangxi of the Qing Dynasty.

Mr Fu Xinian, famous expert in architectural history and professor of Qinghua University, made some interesting findings during his investigations into the relationship between the area of the Forbidden City and its ratios.

Professor Fu first obtained the measurement of the compounds of the Three Rear Palaces: The width from the east to the west is 118 meters and the length from the south to the north 218 meters, the ratio between the two being 6:11. His measurement of the compounds of the Three Grand Halls has indicated the width from the east to the west at 234 meters and the length from the south to the north at 437 meters, the ratio being the same—6:11. The length and width of the latter has almost doubled that of the former, namely, the area of the front court is four times greater than that of the rear palace compound.

On the either side of the Three Rear Palaces there are six palaces and five halls from the east to the west respectively. The measurements Professor Fu has acquired show the length is 216 meters and the width 119 meters, which are on the whole identical to those of the compounds of the Three Rear Palaces.

Professor Fu thinks that the establishment of a feudal empire in China is, to the emperor, a process of "turning a home into a state," and this accounts for the reason why the home of an emperor (the rear palaces) forms the ratio for the planning of the construction of the front three halls and the other architectural structures.

We might thus arrive at the conclusion that in terms of political structure of an ancient empire, a state is an enlarged or extended home, and this notion is also proved in the architectural design of the Forbidden City, where home (rear residence) exceeds state (front court). This analysis has helped in the interpretation, from the perspective of material and cultural history, of the "unity of home and state" philosophy in ancient China.

"Frank and Honest" Plaque and Secret Selection of Successor to the Throne

Inside the Gate of Heavenly Purity, there lies in the middle a paved

The Palace of Heavenly Purity (highest in ranking and largest in size among the rear palaces, with a double eave and hip roof and nine animal sculptures on the corners of the eaves)

The Palace of Earthly Tranquility (a little smaller in size and scale than the Palace of Heavenly Purity, with a double eave and hip roof, but seven animal sculptures on the corners of the eaves)

path of approximately 10 meters wide with white stone rails on either side, leading directly to the Palace of Heavenly Purity.

"Qian" in "Qian Qing Gong" (the Palace of Heavenly Purity) stands for "Heaven," and "Kun" in "Kun Ning Gong" (the Palace of Earthly Tranquility) "Earth." The names of the Palace of Heavenly Purity and the Palace of Earthly Tranquility have remained unchanged ever since the founding of the Forbidden City in the early Ming Dynasty. Enduring peace and prosperity is a long and ever-cherished dream of an emperor.

Sundial, *jialiang*, copper stove, copper crane and copper turtle (all these symbols of power and eternity) are arranged on the red-painted stone terrace in front of the grand hall. A copper temple is set on either side of the stone terrace, which, when put together, is called a Golden Hall of the World.

The Palace of Heavenly Purity is nine bays in width and five bays in

Interior of the Palace of Heavenly Purity

depth. A golden throne carved with dragon patterns is located in the center of the palace, with a golden dragon-patterned screen set behind the dragon chair and *luduan* (divine animal), cranes, and fragrance stands in front. This layout is similar in style and design to that of the Hall of Supreme Harmony. Books, paintings, antiques, and four treasures of the study are also displayed in the Eastern Warm Chamber and the Western Warm Chamber. These exhibits have been restored to their original state.

The most celebrated object in the Palace of Heavenly Purity is the massive horizontal board hanging high up in the palace, with four characters 正大光明 (Frank and Honest). The four characters were originally written by Shunzhi, which were then imitated by Kangxi before being carved onto a plaque. Qianlong later re-copied the characters and had them made onto a plaque. So the characters on the plaque came actually from the handwriting of Qianlong. It is quite remarkable that the three emperors of three different generations were so fond of these four characters.

The throne in the Palace of Heavenly Purity

The Golden Hall of State and the Golden Hall of Power (the Golden Hall of State on the east side, and the Golden Hall of Power on the west side, both halls symbolic of the supremacy of imperial power and authority)

With the passage of time, the formerly white characters on the plaque have now turned yellow. Over the last 200 years, the plaque has paid quiet witness to the numerous ups and downs that have taken place in the palace; and the plaque is inextricably interlinked with a history that is full of mysteries.

The rule of the Qing Dynasty was established by the Manchu, and there were no specified rules formulated for succession to the throne. The Han tradition of the eldest son by wife being the natural successor was not used in this period. The succession of Emperor Shunzhi to the throne resulted from some accidental factors. There were also some non-natural links about the ascendance of Emperor Kangxi to the throne. Kangxi had for a time been hesitant in his decision to choose a successor until finally no ideal candidate could be found. This gave rise to conflicts and fights among his descendants, and eventually Yinchen, his fourth son, came out as a winner and ascended the throne as Emperor Yongzheng. However, rumors that Yongzheng falsified his father's will by changing "... succeeded to the 14th son ..." into "... succeeded to the 4th son ..." were abundant and are still speculated to this day.

Learning from the lessons of history, Yongzheng, after taking over power, stipulated a system of secret succession. The system was operated by a written confidential imperial edict by the emperor in person, which was made in two copies and stored in two boxes, with one copy kept by the emperor in a secret place and the other behind the "Fairness and Honest" plaque. This meant that the successor had already been designated. In the time of need, the two copies were retrieved and compared to avoid possible conflicts and unrest.

On August 23 of the 13th year of Yongzheng reign (October 8, 1735), the emperor died of disease. The ministers took out the box behind

Secret edict of succession to the throne written by Emperor Daoguang and the box for the confidential imperial decree

the plaque and compared the copy with the other. The two copies matched each other exactly. Hongli then ascended to the throne. That was Qianlong, who was fortunate enough to be the first emperor of the Qing Dynasty after the adoption of this system.

In the same way Jiaqing succeeded Qianlong, Daoguang succeeded Jiaqing, and Xianfeng succeeded Daoguang. A copy of confidential imperial edict on throne succession, written personally by Emperor Daoguang, together with a box for the edict, is still under the care of the First Historical Archives of China.

The Hall of Union: Treasured Imperial Seals

The Hall of Union, constructed in the mid-Ming Dynasty, looks very much like the Hall of Central Harmony; characterized by its single–eave square

Interior of the Hall of Union

pavilion shape. However, similarity does not necessarily mean the sameness of the two halls. They each have appeal in their own respective ways.

The Hall of Union is relatively smaller in size—three bays in depth and three bays in width, accessible from the doors on all four sides and quite compact. Critics think the addition of the Hall of Union in between the Palace of Heavenly Purity and the Palace of Earthly Tranquility makes the space cramped and oppressive resulting in a flaw in an otherwise perfect work. In terms of esthetic conceptions of architecture, there are sometimes as many men as opinions.

The name comes from *The Book of Changes*, refers to harmonization in astrology, harmony between the emperor and the empress, unity between the monarch and the ministers, prosperity in society, and luck for people. The golden characters against a blue setting of the plaque over the entrance

Left: A large chiming clock in the Hall of Union (made by the court workmen in 1798, which serves as both a practical item and a valuable appreciation piece which plays pleasant sounds and keeps good time)
Right: Copper clepsydra

are written in Manchu and Chinese languages, the Chinese characters on the left and the Manchu on the right. Most of the steles in the Imperial Palace are patterned in this format and are left over from the Qing Dynasty.

Standing at the entrance, you will see the throne in the center of the hall, over which is a stele with two characters 无为 (let things take their own course), which were originally written by Kangxi and later copied by Qianlong. Kangxi and Qianlong admired the way sage monarch Shun who had ruled over the Yu Kingdom in ancient China, and expected their successors could learn from sage monarch Shun.

At the east side of the Hall of Union stands a copper clepsydra (an ancient device using water to measure the flow of time), and at the west side stands a large chiming clock which was considered a "modern" and "hi-tech" item in the Ming and Qing Dynasties. Because of the presence of the chiming clock, the copper clepsydra has stopped its daily routine ever since Emperor Qianlong. Despite the absence of its practical value, the practice of "copper clepsydra on the left and chiming clock on the right" has remained a patterned mode. The copper clepsydra stays where it has always been as an ornament.

The empress played an important role in the activities taking place in the Hall of Union in the Qing Dynasty. On each empress's birthday, the empress would come to the hall to accept good wishes and blessings from people, including the emperor, the empress dowager, imperial concubines and princes, who acted in compliance with the rules on rites. On the New Year's Day (the first day of the lunar year), the empress would also be present to receive people coming to express greetings or to pay respects.

Beginning from the 13th year of Qianlong (1748), the Hall of Union became an important location for collecting and keeping the emperors' seals. An imperial seal is also called *xi* (玺) or *bao* (宝), which serves as a keepsake from an emperor to his subjects and people in general. An official document issued by the emperor must be annexed thereto with an imperial seal before coming into effect. Cai Yong in the Han Dynasty said in *Arbitrary*, "Ever since the Qin Dynasty, the seal has belonged exclusively to the emperor, and the imperial seal is made exclusively of jade. No official is courageous enough to use a jade seal." A jade seal gradually became a symbol of imperial power beyond access to anyone else. Legend says that the imperial seal in the Qin Dynasty was made of Lantian jade, with Chinese characters carved, expressing a wish of lasting peace and prosperity. Resulting from the impact of the theory of fatality, the imperial seal has taken on a mysterious color and come to be regarded as a treasured dispeller of all evils and an assurance of Heaven's will.

25 imperial seals of the Qing court are stored securely in a cabinet in

Sandalwood "Emperor's Treasure" imperial seal (for crowning an empress), jade imperial seal, and gold imperial seal

the Hall of Union. In order to explain why 25 had been decided on as the number of imperial seals to be stored, Qianlong once wrote in *Treasures in the Hall of Union* that this number accorded with "predestination." He also went on to describe the rules for the application of each seal, and the shape and making of each of the seals. However, it is not until he was 86 that Qianlong disclosed the real idea behind the number 25 set for the imperial seals, which was actually inspired by a story about the Zhou Dynasty. It was inspired by King Ping of Zhou, who moved the capital to Luoyang and started the 25 generations empire of the Eastern Zhou Dynasty. This is the longest empire in terms of generation in the history of China's dynasties. And Qianlong wished the Qing Dynasty could stay just as long as the Eastern Zhou Dynasty. However, despite his use of the number 25, the Qing Dynasty, from Shunzhi to Xuantong, experienced a reign of only 10 generations.

The smallest of the 25 seals is just 6.8 cm in length and width, the largest is19.2 cm in width, the highest 14.8 cm and the shortest 6 cm. The seals are made of jade, gold or sandalwood, acquiring various names for applications to various documents.

Palace of Earthly Tranquility: Grand Imperial Wedding

As was originally planned, the Palace of Heavenly Purity and the Palace of Earthly Tranquility were to be built alike, the former being the residing palace of the emperor and the latter of the empress. The Palace of Earthly Tranquility, which is nine bays in width and seven bays in length, served as residential quarters for almost all the empresses during the Ming Dynasty. Towards the end of the Ming Dynasty, Li Zicheng led his troops into the city and captured Beijing. The Empress Zhou, wife of Emperor Chongzhen, committed suicide there.

Kangxi's wedding was held in the Palace of Heavenly Purity. He was then 12 years old, and the empress only 13. Nine years later, the empress died in the Palace of Earthly Tranquility from excess bleeding after labor. The succeeding empress also took her residence in the Palace of Earthly Tranquility, but died of disease in less than six months.

Starting with Yongzheng, emperors of the Qing Dynasty moved to live in the Hall of Mental Cultivation, and their empresses no longer dwelt in the Palace of Earthly Tranquility. Some of the rooms in the west of the palace were once transformed into shamans' sacrificial spots, where

The interior of the main hall of the Palace of Earthly Tranquility (a sacrificial ceremony was held here in the Qing Dynasty on December 23 each year, when the emperor would be personally present)

The Eastern Warm Chamber of the Palace of Earthly Tranquility

images or statues of god and sacrificial utensils are still seen.

In the Qing Dynasty, the two rooms in the east of the Palace of Earthly Tranquility were long employed as a bridal chamber for the emperor and the empress. Shunzhi, Kangxi, Tongzhi, Guangxu and Puyi all used the bridal chamber, which was popularly known as the Eastern Warm Chamber. Since many of the emperors in the Qing Dynasty were married before ascending to the throne, not all the newly-weds had to move to live in here. The furnishings as observed today are restored from the original used when Guangxu's wedding took place.

The wedding ceremony of Guangxu was the grandest occasion in the court history of the Qing Dynasty. It also serves as a great representation of the wedding of an emperor in the imperial history in China. That took place in the year 1889, when the political situation was severe and the entire empire was faced with both trouble from within, and attack from without. However, the imperial court spared no effort in making the wedding unprecedented and spent a total of five million ounces of silver on the celebration.

On January 27, 1889, the 22-year-old Longyu, niece of Cixi, knelt down in front of the lobby of her own home, and listened to the special envoy of Emperor Guangxu announce the imperial edict entitling her as empress. She then accepted the imperial edict and the seal. With the help of two palace maids, she climbed into the phoenix sedan chair, and, accompanied by a guard of honor and a drum corps, set out for the imperial palace. That day, the entire city was decked out with lanterns and colorful streamers. The sedan chair went through the Meridian Gate and entered the Gate of Heavenly Purity before halting under the eaves of the Palace of Heavenly Purity. The empress then changed into a peacock-topped sedan chair carried by eight people, heading toward the Palace of Accumulated Purity of the Six Eastern Palaces, where the empress had a brief rest and perfected her some make-up.

At 5 o'clock in the afternoon, the empress got on the peacock-topped sedan chair again and arrived at the red-carpet-floored Eastern Warm Chamber in the Palace of Earthly Tranquility. As the empress and all those present waited respectfully, the emperor arrived in his wedding costume. The emperor and the empress then seated themselves on the wedding bed, and ate *zisun bobo* (small dumplings prepared specially for the bride and bridegroom) before moving over to the *kang* (a heatable brick bed) in the south, sitting side-by-side, with the emperor on the left and the empress on the right. The newlywed began their wedding ceremony by drinking from

Partial picture of the grand wedding ceremony of Emperor Guangxu (a scene of the grand wedding at the Hall of Supreme Harmony)

the nuptial cup. Drinking from the nuptial cup is unlike what is commonly called *jiaobeijiu* (drinking from each other's cup), and it is merely of a ceremonial nature. After that, they ate longevity noodles. Early the next morning (the 28th), a Gather-together Banquet was given.

For three days after their wedding, Guangxu and his empress stayed together in the Eastern Warm Chamber in the Palace of Earthly Tranquility. The emperor then returned to the Hall of Mental Cultivation and the empress moved to the Hall of State Satisfaction to the east of the Hall of Mental Cultivation.

Emperor Guangxu's wedding unfolded on a grand and spectacular scale. However, the couple was not on amicable terms thereafter, which had a negative impact upon the political situation in the late Qing Dynasty.

Privy Council: Major Military and Political Decision-making Authority

There is a row of single-storey houses along the wall in the north of the Gate of Glorifying Forebears, of which five belonged to the well-known Privy Council.

It is necessary to trace back to the ancient system of prime minister and cabinet in China before explaining the status and function of the Privy Council.

The system of prime minister was initiated in the Spring and Autumn Period and the Warring States Period, and became established in the Qin and Han Dynasties. The duty of a prime minister was to serve the emperor, yet he stood above all the other officials, holding in hand an extreme power. This may well account for the long existent and insoluble contradictions and conflicts in power between emperors and prime ministers. After the formation of the Ming Dynasty, Zhu Yuanzhang appropriated all power to himself, abolishing the system of prime minister that had been handed down for one thousand and eight or nine hundred years.

Zhu Yuanzhang selected talented officials to serve in the imperial court to assist him in the state affairs, who were famed as Court Scholars. On this basis, a "cabinet" system began to take shape. According to this system, the cabinet members participated in the administration of state affairs as well as in decision-making, but were not in charge of the six ministries. The extent and limit of their power was to be decided by the emperor. The replacement of a system of cabinet for that of prime minister indicated a growing acceleration of an autocratic imperial power.

In the early Qing Dynasty, Duoergun, Ao Bai, Suoetu, and Mingzhu assumed dictatorial power one after another.

Former location of the Privy Council (a duty place for officials of the Privy Council, which is separated by a wall from the buildings of the Hall of Mental Cultivation and one hundred meters away from the dwelling place of the emperor, an indication of "closeness" to the imperial authority)

To reinforce the imperial power, emperors including Kangxi formulated their respective novelty. In the 8th year of Yongzheng reign (1739) the Privy Council was officially established, an office handling confidential military and political affairs. The office appointed its own ministers, took charge of the national administrative affairs, and enjoyed more power than either the cabinet or the six ministries.

The Privy Council is described by some as a specialized power organ that was not an office under a legal, independent government but subject directly to the instructions of the emperor. It had no official location (except for a place for duties), no regular office members, no specially-assigned officials and no subordinates. All its members, sometimes two or three in number and sometimes seven or eight, were selected personally by the emperor from among the princes and important ministers, holding two or more positions concurrently. This structure formed a vital part in the Qing government.

The Privy Council was an outer-and-outer dependency, performing humbly every instruction as issued by the emperor to the letter. Mr. Jiang Min, an expert in the history of China's navy and friend of the author's,

Portrait of Emperor Yongzheng (having taken a series of measures to strengthen his imperial power, striking cabals, eliminating political enemies, reforming the system of officials and going in for literary inquisition energetically)

has been to the Imperial Palace a great number of times and has specially observed the row of single-storey houses along the wall in the north of the Gate of Glorifying Forebears with interest. Mr. Jiang wrote in his prose "Tour to Privy Council," "These ministers were of extreme power, and yet in the eye of an emperor, they were nothing but servants. The office is unimaginably shabby and simple. There is a heatable brick bed against a wall, taking up half the space in the room. A few chairs and desks are placed there and the furniture is covered with a gray cover of accumulated dust. The ceiling-covered roof makes the room feel low, in striking contrast with the tall mysterious palaces. On the east wall hangs a plaque with the characters 喜报红旌 (good news red flag) inscribed by Emperor Xianfeng ... In my impression, the Privy Council has never been open to tourists. Each time I visited the place, I had to peep from the blurring window glass into the dark inside ..."

Today, the former houses of the Privy Council have been made into an exhibition hall, and display historical documents of the Privy Council.

Office for Administering Eunuchs: A Distorted Men's World

The single-storey houses in the west of the Gate of Heavenly Purity are

The former locations of the South Study and the Office for Administering Eunuchs

known as Nan Shu Fang (the Southern Study) and Jing Shi Fang (the Office for Administering Eunuchs) in the Qing Dynasty. The former used to be the location where scholars from the Imperial Academy attended to the emperor, assisting the emperor in drafting an imperial decree, accompanying the emperor in recitation and composition of poems, or offering advice on state affairs. The emperor might make use of these occasions as a means to determine the ability and behavior of an official. Young Kangxi captured Ao Bai, an influential minister, by this strategy right here in this house, removing a major obstacle in assuming the reigns of government.

At the east end towards the Southern Study is the former location of the supervisory department in the Qing Dynasty, called the Office for Administering Eunuchs. One might feel, when looking into the Office for Administering Eunuchs, as if they have seen again this special group of men working there in those days in this Imperial Palace.

The Office for Administering Eunuchs was subject to the administration of the Ministry of Internal Affairs, taking charge of the eunuchs in the Palace. The eunuch is also called *huanguan*, *yanren*, *zhongquan*, or *neijian*. For reasons of various natures, they received the same physiological and surgical operation: castration–removal of testicles, which in ancient China was known as *gongxing* (palace punishment). These men were of a special value in the emperor's eye, and were thus assigned to take charge of managerial and service work. It is not hard to imagine what could have happened if normal men had replaced the eunuchs in a palace where there gathered hundreds of concubines and palace maids. The formation of eunuchs as a special group of people could well help to check the occurrence of "licentious conduct" in the Palace and ensure the purity of the blood of the imperial family. This special group has also contributed to a unique court culture and a social phenomenon of a typical Chinese character.

Eunuchs at a time exercised significant influence upon the political affairs in the Ming Dynasty. Some of them allowed themselves to commit crimes and evils and even override the authority of an emperor. In the Zhengde years, Liu Jin appropriated all power to himself and many ministers addressed him very respectively. These ministers even lowered their own status to such an extent as to call themselves boy servants. At that time, there were said to have been two emperors: one sitting emperor and the other standing emperor, the former Emperor Zhu and the latter Emperor Liu.

During Tianqi's reign, Wei Zhongxian would like to be addressed as His Royal Highness. To please him, local officials competed in building up memorial halls everywhere in his honor. One day in the 17th year of Emperor Chenghua (1481), Ah Chou, a court clown, pretended to be drunk in his performance for the emperor, and said intentionally, "I don't know there's such a person as emperor. What I know is there's a eunuch by the name of Wang." The eunuch was then an extremely powerful military commander Wang Zhi, who formed his own clique to pursue his selfish interests and perpetrated numerous evils. But all these warned the emperor that he should never let go of his imperial power.

Rulers in the early Qing Dynasty came to notice such serious developments and decided to stipulate rules to bring the eunuchs under strict control. The humble status of a eunuch was regulated by state laws and ancestral systems. During Shunzhi's reign, a special iron notice board was erected in the Hall of Union, specifying that eunuchs should stand by to be summoned only for services and should not interfere in state affairs. During Kangxi's reign, the Office for Administering Eunuchs was formed, responsible for the handling of affairs within the palace in accordance with the emperor's instructions.

After the reign of Emperor Xianfeng, things changed for the worse. Cixi forged an indissoluble bond with the eunuchs, with Li Lianying and Xiao Dezhang as representatives. They banded together, wrecking the country and ruining the people. In the game of court politics, the Office for Administering Eunuchs played an irreplaceable role.

Lu Xun once pointed out that the system of eunuchs in the palace and foot-binding among women constituted two evils in ancient times

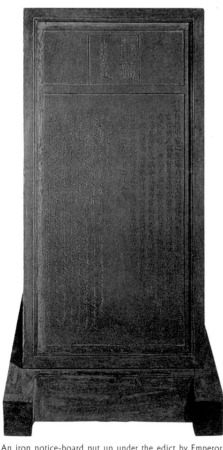

An iron notice-board put up under the edict by Emperor Shunzhi (mandating that the eunuch shall not interfere in state affairs, and those who should act against this rule shall be punished by death)

Ship model of a vessel in Zheng He's fleet (According to the legend, Zheng He was a witted and courageous man, admired and respected by people all over the world.)

of China. From the perspective of the sufferings of individuals, eunuchs underwent physiological distortions and psychological ruins. They were reduced to pathetic victims of imperial power and politics, inferior in social position. A few of them spared no effort in pleasing their emperors and, for a time, won favor from them. They manipulated power and become extremely arrogant, bringing crisis and chaos to the imperial authority. In the course of the rise and fall of an ancient empire in China, the intensifying monopoly of power and aggravating periodical interference in state affairs by eunuchs left a deep imprint upon the minds of people like a shadow that can never be eliminated.

Of the eunuchs of the past dynasties, some are notorious and cheap in moral integrity. However, there are distinguished figures, which have long been remembered in history, like Cai Lun and Zheng He. Zheng He, who, as a eunuch, walked out of the Forbidden City and led his fleet, navigating seven times across seas from 1405 to 1430, made tremendous contributions, as a great navigator in the world's history, to the economic and cultural exchange between the Chinese people and Asian-African peoples.

Fairness and Benevolence: Ideal or Signboard
—A Visit to West Road and East Road

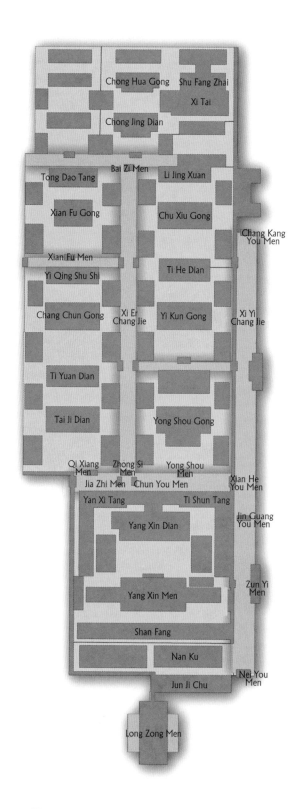

Plan of the West Road of the Three Rear Palaces

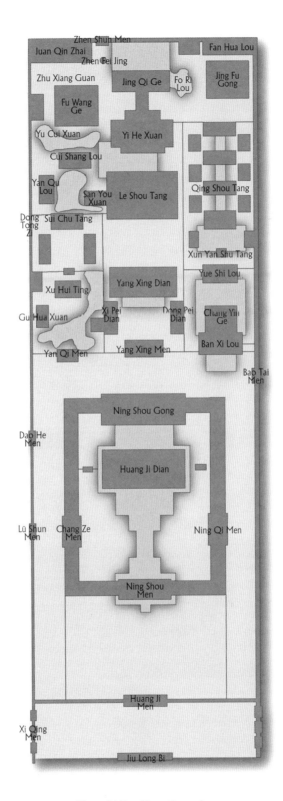

Plan of Ning Shou Gong Area

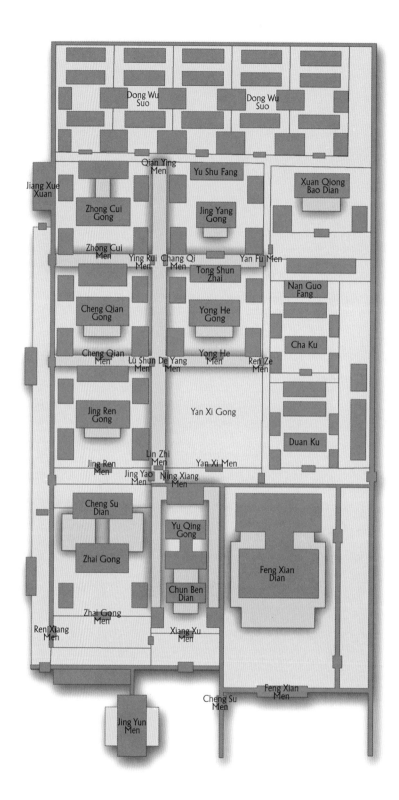

Plan of the East Road of the Three Rear Palaces

Hall of Mental Cultivation: How?

Walk out of Yue Hua Men (the Gate of Luminous Moon) to the west of the Three Rear Palaces and you come to the West Road. To make things easier, we shall put the Inner Court to the west of the Three Palaces and the Outer West Road together, and call them in a general term as West Road. Similarly, East Road refers to the palace group to the east of the Three Palaces including the so-called Outer East Road.

The West No. 1 Street runs across from south to north outside of the Gate of Luminous Moon. The southern end of the long street is the Right Inner Gate, which leads to the Gate of Heavenly Purity Square. On both sides of this seven-meter-wide long street stand Zun Yi Men (the Gate of Obeying Morality and Justice) and the Gate of Luminous Moon, which are opposite each other. Behind the Gate of Obeying Morality and Justice lies a group of buildings known as the Hall of Mental Cultivation, which are composed of Yang Xin Men (the Gate of Mental Cultivation), the Hall of Mental Cultivation and the rear hall of the Hall of Mental Cultivation.

Of all the architectural structures, the Hall of Mental Cultivation ranks among the best-known in the Imperial Palace, next to the Front Three Halls

The Gate of Mental Cultivation (Standing outside the gate, one has an awesome feeling. A wooden screen stands right inside the gate with two doors that may be opened or closed, which adds more mystery to the mysterious.)

Outdoor scene of the Hall of Mental Cultivation (Emperors used to meet their ministers individually in the Western Warm Chamber for confidential reasons.)

and the Three Rear Palaces, simply because eight emperors after Emperor Yongzheng of the Qing Dynasty were here attending to the state affairs and taking their residences. In addition, many an important historical event originated here or came to the fore, and it is here where three emperors (Shunzhi, Qianlong and Tongzhi) of the Qing Dynasty concluded their life.

In 1722, Emperor Kangxi died of disease in Chang Chun Yuan (the Garden of Exhilarating Spring, located near the west gate of Beijing University today). The succeeding Emperor Yongzheng observed mourning for the deceased emperor in the Hall of Mental Cultivation. Since then, Yongzheng never moved back to the Palace of Heavenly Purity to live, turning the Hall of Mental Cultivation into his own dwelling place, while the Palace of Heavenly Purity was used for court audiences and the storage of secret box for the confidential imperial decree.

Yongzheng moved into the Hall of Mental Cultivation with the superficial reason to reminisce his forefathers and to avoid the scene that invariably brought back past memories. From the perspective of architectural science, the Hall of Mental Cultivation was a good choice for living quarters. Compared with the Palace of Heavenly Purity, the Hall of Mental

Left: The Hall of Mental Cultivation Proper (The Hall, with court desk and an imperial throne, serves as a location where the emperor in the Qing Dynasty would meet his ministers, and officials as well.)

Cultivation is less magnificent, but is free from a certain kind of rigidity and dullness. We can conclude that this was also an important reason behind Yongzheng's decision.

Mental cultivation refers to a *gongfu* (an effort) applied by the ancients in their cultivation of mind, with emphasis on the refining of one's sentiment. Mengzi, Chinese philosopher and one of the greatest Confucian scholars, said, "To cultivate one's mind is to curtail one's desires." It is only natural that to expect an emperor to curtail all his desires, required too much of an emperor.

Over the screen is a plaque with four characters: 中正仁和 (fairness and benevolence) inscribed by Yongzheng, which best reveals and summarizes the lofty realm of thought in the emperor.

However, how far did any of these "masters" in the Forbidden City ever so earnestly practice and live up to what they had been committed to or advocated? It is evident that some did so, to greater degrees than others.

The Eastern Warm Chamber: Attending Court Affairs from behind a Screen

The Hall of Mental Cultivation actually is of three bays, which are partitioned by square columns into nine bays. This is intended to make it conform to the imperial throne. A veranda is extended out from the front eave of the main bay and the subordinate bay in the west. The front chamber and the rear chamber are joined by a short porch. The rear chamber was the dwelling of the emperor, which is yet another instance of the imperial rule of "court in the front, home at the back." To the east of the rear chamber is Ti Shun Tang (the Hall of State Satisfaction), where the empress took her residence each time she came to the Hall of Mental Cultivation to keep the emperor company. To the west of the rear chamber is Yan Xi Tang (the Hall of Auspicious Swallow), where the imperial concubine spent nights with the emperor each time he came to the Hall of Mental Cultivation.

Visitors to the Hall of Mental Cultivation will not fail to stop at the Eastern Warm Chamber (auxiliary chamber in the east) of the front hall to take a close look through the window at the scene of "attending to state affairs from behind a screen." In China, stories about "attending to state affairs from behind a screen" and the attending Empress Dowager Cixi are known to every household.

In the summer of 1861, Emperor Xianfeng died. His six-year-old son succeeded him and became Emperor Tongzhi. Before his death, Xianfeng gave order that Sushun and other seven senior ministers assist, as minister-regents, the young emperor in the administration of state affairs. However, he gave his imperial seal to the empress (Empress Dowager Cian) and his "Tong Dao Tang" seal to the crown prince. It was then stipulated that none of the imperial decrees jointly endorsed by the eight senior ministers was of any effect without the imperial seal and the "Tong Dao Tang" seal annexed thereto. The idea behind such arrangement resulted from the consideration that an inter-containing effect could thus be achieved. On the one hand the imperial concubines would have no chance to usurp the power and on the other hand, the minister-regents would not be in a position to

The Eastern Warm Chamber in the Hall of Mental Cultivation (In those days, the emperor was sitting before the screen and the empress dowager Cixi behind the screen, conducting court affairs. Cixi seized power entirely, making decisions and ruling over China for 48 years.)

exclusively seize the power.

However, in the autumn of 1861 Cixi, who had been highly respected as Empress Dowager and equal in title to Cian as "empress dowager of the two palaces," resolutely staged a coup d'etat, put the eight senior ministers to death, reformed the Privy Council and placed the political program under her control. Soon, a memorandum was presented to the emperor on "Rules Regarding Administering State Affairs from behind a Screen." Cixi was only too glad to accept it, and thereby began to practice attendance to state affairs from behind a screen with Cian in the Eastern Warm Chamber.

What happened was that a screen was put up with the emperor sitting before the screen and the two empress dowagers of the two palaces Cixi and Cian behind the screen, conducting court affairs. Cian was not good at political affairs, and was, by nature, kind and generous, so the actual power was tightly held in the hands of Cixi.

In 1873, Emperor Tongzhi came to the age of 18, and declared that he would personally take care of the court affairs. Cixi then had to remove the screen and release her hold on power. Less than two years later, Tongzhi contracted smallpox and died of the disease. Tongzhi had no son to succeed to the throne, and was the only son of Emperor Xianfeng, so Cixi, who was so anxious to again control the power and who was so skilled in resorting to every artifice, designated, without any consent or authority, the cousin of Tongzhi and the son of her full sister and Prince Chun to take over the imperial throne. The successor was at that time only four years old and later became Emperor Guangxu. Cixi selected the youngster of the same generation as Tongzhi instead of one a generation junior to Tongzhi so as to justify herself in continuing her attendance of state affairs from behind a screen, or else the assistance to the young emperor would fall as by right upon the empress of Emperor Tongzhi.

Portrait of Guangxu (Guangxu ascended to the throne at the age of four, remaining a mere puppet before the age of 16. Guangxu intended to do something great after taking over power, yet luck and wisdom were not in his favor. At the age of 28, he was reduced to a mere "prisoner.")

Portrait of Empress Dowager Cixi (Cixi was the empress of Xianfeng and biological mother of Tongzhi. After the death of Xianfeng, Cixi broke up the traditional rule of women being forbidden to interfere in the state affairs, becoming the actual ruler of China.)

For the second time, Cixi began to sit behind the screen in the Eastern Warm Chamber. In 1881 Cian passed away from a disease, and Cixi was the only one left behind the screen. The original scene has now been restored in the Eastern Warm Chamber.

After Guangxu assumed the reigns, Cixi for a time retired from court affairs to the Summer Palace, but started her third round of attendance as a result of the Reform Movement in 1898, when she put Guangxu under house arrest at Ying Tai (Sea Terrace Islet) in Zhong and Nan Hai, until her death. This time, the screen was no longer in demand and she was seated at the throne with Guangxu sitting beside her. The ministers present at the court would face Cixi, who would call this as "administration by instructions."

Refined Taste of a Ruler

A small house to the south windows of the Western Warm Chamber of the Hall of Mental Cultivation is the much-celebrated San Xi Tang (the Room of Three Rarities or the Room of Three Hopes). San Xi Tang may be defined in two ways: 1. The so-called concept of "a learned man hopes to be a man of virtue, a man of virtue hopes to be a wise man, and a wise man hopes to be Heaven" embodies a spirit of motivation and ambition; and 2. Xi (希, hope) synonymous to xi (稀, rarity), refers to the three rare treasures collected here—three great calligraphy models in the history of China's calligraphy by Wang Xizhi, calligrapher of the Eastern Jin Dynasty, Wang Xianzhi, calligrapher of the Eastern Jin Dynasty, and Wang Xun, Chinese calligrapher. Emperor Qianlong had a keen interest in calligraphy and painting, and a literary quality about him as well. Qianlong was extremely happy to have acquired these copies, which he kept in his study he frequented almost every day, and later he renamed the study. Of course, Heaven was what he claimed himself to be.

The Room of Three Raristies is approximately eight square meters in area, partitioned into two smaller rooms of four square meters each. Thanks to its intricate design and delicate arrangement, these small spaces, however, do not impress people as cramped, and, instead,

The Room of Three Rarities

Cup Floating Channel in the Pavilion of Ceremonial Purification

they look brightly-lit. Its decoration is elegantly requisite, contributing to the hall being a location of extraordinarily unique design and taste. A horizontal board is hung over the entrance inscribed with the characters of 三希堂 (the Room of Three Rarities) written personally by Qianlong. The board is joined by an antithetical couplet hanging down on both sides.

The esthetic mood of Qianlong is also perceived in the Qianlong Garden, which is located in the northwest corner of Ning Shou Gong (the Palace of Tranquility and Longevity) Area, also known as the Ning Shou Gong Garden. The garden

The Pavilion of Pleasant Sounds (the biggest stage in the Forbidden City, situated in the Ning Shou Gong Area, found in the 37th year of Qianlong)

designers have demonstrated their skills in their refined design and clever composition in creating such fascinating scenery where a winding path leads to a secluded spot on a narrow strip of land, 160 meters long from south to north and 49 meters long from east to west; which is in the neighborhood of a high wall on the west side and a palace on the east side.

Once inside the garden through Yan Qi Men (the Gate of Spreading Happiness), you will see the garden surrounded by rocks hills and tall ancient trees. Right in the middle of the first courtyard is a pavilion called Gu Hua Xuan (the Pavilion of Old Flowers), and there is a unique pavilion by the name of Xi Shang that corresponds to the Pavilion of Old Flowers

Yue Shi Lou (the Building for Viewing Performances) (north to the Pavilion of Pleasant Sounds where emperors enjoyed drama performances and drinking)

to the west, contributing to a harmonious scenic sight. In Xi Shang Ting (the Pavilion of Ceremonial Purification) a winding, circular water trough has been dug out of the stone floor, and is called Cup Floating Channel. Qianlong was enthusiastic about Wang Xizhi's prose "Lanting Pavilion," imitating a recreational spot where he let a cup float on the water surface in the trough while drinking with his ministers. When the cup floated up to and stopped in front of anyone, he would have to compose a poem, and would have to be penalized with a cup of wine in case of failure to respond as due.

At the northernmost point of the Qianlong Garden is an exquisite two-storied building—Juan Qin Zhai (the Room for Diligent Retired Life). Entertaining himself with folk tunes became the most favored aspect of life in Qianlong's late years. Thereafter, Qing emperors all followed Qianlong's example, and turned out to be lovers of drama performances. Listening to folk music and seeing drama performances after administering state affairs formed an important part of their recreational activities. However, such esthetic moments could many times be disturbed by worries related to state affairs.

Six Palaces: Origin and Reality

Practice of polygamy was popular among the noble classes in ancient China, and the tradition of imperial concubines as reflected in the marriages of emperors was quite typical. Stories of an emperor having "72 concubines in three palaces and six chambers," as passed down from generation to generation, are in some sense a vivid portrayal of such practice.

There are six palaces on both the east side and the west side of the Three Rear Palaces of the Imperial Palace. They are Jing Ren Gong (the Palace of Great Benevolence), Cheng Qian Gong (Palace of Celestial Favor), Zhong Cui Gong (the Palace of Accumulated Purity), Yan Xi Gong (the Palace of Prolonging Happiness), Yong He Gong (the Palace of Eternal Harmony), and Jing Yang Gong (the Palace of Great Brilliance) on the east and Yong Shou Gong (the Palace of Eternal Longevity), Yi Kun Gong (the Palace of Upholding Earth), Chu Xiu Gong (the Palace of Gathered Elegance), Tai Ji Dian (the Hall of Supreme Principle), Chang Chun Gong (the Palace of Eternal Spring) and Xian Fu Gong (the Palace of Universal Happiness) on the west. It is not difficult to notice, when you are moving among

Interior of the Palace of Eternal Spring

Night scene of the West No. 2 Street

these palaces, that the six palaces on either side are arranged in parallel in accordance with square patterns. Each palace forms a self-contained and independent compound, about 50 meters in width and length respectively, with a central axial line of its own. The gate to the courtyard is set in the middle with a screen wall inside facing the gate. The palace is divided into two parts, known as "front halls and back dwelling chambers." Auxiliary halls and wing houses are built on either side of the main hall. Ti Yuan Dian (the Hall of State Unity) and Ti He Dian (the Hall of State Harmony) as we see them today were constructed in the late Qing Dynasty, and the original gate, wall and back hall were for this purpose removed. This has more or less altered the initial established pattern of design.

The six palaces on either side occupy an area of 35% of the total area of the rear court, larger than the Three Rear Palaces. The adoption of the number "six" is related to the stipulation as specified in *The Book of Rites*, according to which the emperor is described to have, aside from the empress, three wives, nine imperial concubines, twenty-seven concubines and eighty-one imperial maids. Six Palaces was later referred to, in general terms, as residential quarters for empress and concubines.

Zhong Si Men (the Katydid Gate) (Zhongsi, an insect, easy in breeding, used by Cixi as a reminder to Guangxu to strive to have more children)

Imperial concubines lived all the year round in seclusion from outside contacts, performing their duties of giving birth to and rearing children for their emperor so that the throne could be passed on to future generations. In the Ming Dynasty, red lanterns would be hung up in the front of each mansion when the curtain of night was falling, expecting in full confidence for the favor of their emperor. Yet, many times they were disappointed. The emperor would choose randomly a mansion to spend the night in, and the red lantern in front of that mansion would then be taken off. The copper lanterns along East No. 1 Street, East No. 2 Street, West No. 1 Street and West No. 2 Street would stay lighted till the approach of dawn.

As an expression of a strong wish for more descendents in the royal family, the names of some streets and gates in the Six Eastern Palaces and the Six Western Palaces are also related to Procreation and Proliferation such as Zhong Si, Bai Zi, Lin Zhi, and Qian Ying. The fertility of the Qing emperors after Xianfeng noticeably declined. Fewer or even no descendants were present to help the system of designation of an heir come to an eventual conclusion. This in turn had a very profound effect on the development of the political situation in the late Qing Dynasty. Good wishes are invariably incapable of resisting an unsympathetic reality.

With the impact of the Manchu traditions, rules for imperial concubines in Qing Dynasty took on some new characteristics. First, imperial concubines were smaller in number. Second, the position of a concubine was higher, demonstrating a clear class distinction in comparison with other maids in the palace. Third, admonishments and restrictions were more severe. The decrease in number of imperial concubines made it possible that the empress and the empress dowager were able to reside here.

Palace of Gathered Elegance: Dignity of Empress Dowager Cixi

Cixi was entitled Worthy Lady Yi (a concubine of the fifth rank) after

Main hall of the Palace of Gathered Elegance (The throne is placed in the middle with evergreen bonsai in green jide pots arranged on either side to indicate the everlasting prosperity of the Qing Dynasty)

her entry into the palace, residing in the Palace of Gathered Elegance. She was also named Worthy Lady Lan simply because of the character 兰 (*lan*) in her name. According to the Qing rules, the empress took care of the imperial residential palace and was in charge of the six palaces, the high-ranking imperial concubines of seven ranks including high-ranking imperial concubines of one highest-ranking imperial concubine, two higher-ranking imperial concubines, four imperial concubines, as well as lower-ranking imperial concubines of Guiren (Worthy Lady), Changzai, and Daying. With her resourcefulness and her special "contribution" of giving birth to a son for Emperor Xianfeng, Cixi rose in her status from Worthy Lady Lan, to Corcubine Yi, Imperial Concubine Yi and eventually to an Empress.

During this period, Cixi also dwelt in the Palace of Eternal Spring

East chamber of the Palace of Gathered Elegance (luxuriously and intricately decorated, with many treasures collected as gifts on the 50th birthday of Cixi)

and other places, and moved back to the Palace of Gathered Elegance at the age of 49 (1883), where she indulged herself in an extravagant arrangement for her 50th birthday celebration. The interior furnishings of the Palace of Gathered Elegance today are a reproduction of the original as documented.

Preparation for this grand occasion started a year earlier when renovations of the Palace of Gathered Elegance, the Palace of Upholding Earth and the Hall of State Harmony went under way. Cixi decided that the Palace of Upholding Earth should be the spot where birthday congratulations and gifts were to be accepted, and that the Hall of State Harmony should be the location where feasts were to be held. Her bedroom was set at the Western Warm Chamber of the Palace of Gathered Elegance. The bedding was all made of embroidered silk fabrics, and the screens and curtains of colored silk fabrics embroidered in Suzhou style. The furniture in the palace was made of hard wood like red sandalwood and rosewood. The ornaments and furnishings were all expensive art crafts such as intricately-carved ivory dragon-boats. The Palace of Gathered Elegance ranks top among all the other palaces in terms of luxury and extravagance.

Color paintings in Suzhou style were Cixi's favorite; like those of flowers, birds, fish and insects; mountains, rivers and human figures; and vegetables and fruits, as well as fairy tales. They were applied to the external eaves of the Palace of Gathered Elegance. The checked doors and windows were made of Chinese cedar (a durable soft wood) and ornamented with patterns expressing wishes for a long life. A pair of copper sculptures of dragons playing with pearls and a pair of copper sculptures of sika deer were erected in the courtyard. The columns of the corridors on the left and the right sides were

Upper: Ivory mat
Lower: Crystal wine vessel

Copper dragons at the Palace of Gathered Elegance (There were unusually placed two copper dragons in the courtyard, which expressed Cixi's intended pursuit of power. Is this an expression that she herself is the Son of Heaven?)

carved by the ministers with words of praise and congratulations as well as wishes for a long life.

Cixi's 50th birthday celebration cost a total of 630,000 ounces of silver. In those days, China was in the midst of domestic trouble and foreign invasion, flames of war were incessant, and the people were experiencing times of great need.

Cixi was keen on face-saving and fond of extravagance and waste. This was not merely a result of her vanity and love of comfort, but rather, a motive intended to build up her own dignity and power.

Such maternal domination did indeed prove to be a disaster to the average people and the entire nation alike.

The Hall for Abstinence

Small Forbidden City: Scheme to Be a "Super-emperor"

Zhai Gong (the Hall for Abstinence) is located inside Ren Xiang Men (the Gate of Benevolence and Auspiciousness) along the East No. 1 Street, to the south of the six palaces on the east side. Upon an important sacrificial ceremony, emperors in the Qing Dynasty would come here to stay a while, practicing religious abstinence before proceeding to the worshipping. During the period, emperors would compose themselves, keeping away from meat dishes, alcoholic drinks, recreational activities and sexual desires.

Feng Xian Men (the Gate for Ancestral Worship)

To the east of the Hall for Abstinence is Yu Qing Gong (the Palace of the Bringing-forth of Blessings), across from which is the Hall for Ancestral Worship. The place where memorial tablets for the royal ancestors were enshrined in the Qing Dynasty is called Inner Imperial Ancestral Temple. To the east of the Hall for Ancestral Worship runs a long street by the name of Dong Tong Zi (the East Long Passage).

To the east of the East Long Passage is the Ning Shou Gong Area, covering the entire building group of the Hall of Great Supremacy, the Palace of Tranquility and Longevity, Yang Xing Dian (the Hall of Spiritual Cultivation), and Le Shou Tang (the Hall of Joyful Longevity). Emperor Qianlong spent more than one million four hundred thousand ounces of silver reconstructing these structures, which were intended to serve as imperial residences when he became the "super-emperor" after being an

Nine-Dragon Screen (a glazed-tiled screen with nine dragons of different bearings, corresponding to which are another nine dragons on the ridge of the hall roof)

emperor for sixty years.

The Ning Shou Gong Area is accessible by Xi Qing Men (the Gate of Thriving Royal House) close to the south end of the East Long Passage (today Treasure Hall as shown on the gate), and the courtyard is just across the Gate of Great Supremacy. On the southern wall of the courtyard is inlaid a delicate and colorful Nine-dragon Screen directly facing the Gate of Great Supremacy. The great yellow dragon in the middle of the screen falls on the south-north central axial line with the Gate of Great Supremacy, Ning Shou Men (the Gate of Tranquility and Longevity), the Hall of Great Supremacy, the Palace of Tranquility and Longevity, the Hall of Spiritual Cultivation, and the Hall of Joyful Longevity, displaying the tremendous momentum of the small forbidden city.

The Hall of Great Supremacy is the main hall of this "imperial palace

The Hall of Great Supremacy

of the imperial palaces," constructed in imitation of the Hall of Supreme Harmony, with a double eave and hip roof. The hall, however, has only seven bays to indicate that it is one rank inferior to the Hall of Supreme Harmony. The Palace of Tranquility and Longevity is imitated from the Palace of Earthly Tranquility, and both have seven bays. Nevertheless, the approach of building seven bays plus the surrounding corridors on the left and the right sides was adopted in the construction of the Hall of Great Supremacy and the Palace of Tranquility and Longevity. So, nine bays were actually built. This was a clear indication as to how hard the "super-emperor" had thought over his plan and how ostentatious the "super-emperor" had been.

On January 4 of the first year of Emperor Jiaqing (1796), Qianlong, as "super-emperor," presided over the second Thousand Aged Banquet at the Hall of Great Supremacy (the first was held in the 50th year of Qianlong) to mark his successful "resumption of throne." More than five thousand male over 60 year olds were invited to the banquet of over eight hundred dining tables, where 3497 poems were collected. This might be the

The Hall of Joyful Longevity (The Hall is located behind the Hall of Spiritual Cultivation, and about 600 servants were here, waiting upon Cixi in those years. In August 1900, Cixi held Guangxu under duress, fleeing away from here.)

exclusive and most unprecedented grand occasion the Forbidden City has ever witnessed in its long history. During the banquet praises would have flooded one's ears. Qianlong was in a great mood, awarding the official accessories of the seventh rank to the aged over 90 and, as a special treat, the official accessories of the sixth rank to 106-year-old Xiong Guopei and 100-year-old Qiu Chenglong. Traditional custom and imperial politics were at this point smartly combined and manipulated by Qianlong.

However, after the creation of the new myth of abdication of throne, Qianlong actually did not move to the Palace of Tranquility and Longevity and, instead, stayed at the Hall of Mental Cultivatuon, handling his state of affairs. Qianlong had not even stayed a single night at the Hall of Spiritual Cultivation, which was constructed after the Hall of Mental Cultivation of the Forbidden City. Even though the title of the reigning emperor had changed to Jiaqing, almanacs were made all the same in both the 61st and the 62nd year of Qianlong.

It was not until Qianlong died in the Hall of Mental Cultivation three years later that Jiaqing became the master of the Hall of Mental Cultivation, exercising the rights that now belonged to him.

Many years later, Cixi settled on this small forbidden city Qianlong had conceived. She went against the traditional Qing rules and moved out of Ci Ning Gong (the Palace of Compassion and Tranquility), a residence for the emperor's mother, known as the Old Widow's House and into the Western Warm Chamber of the Hall of Joyful Longevity, beginning to be the Empress Dowager of the Qing Dynasty.

A plan that had been conceived a hundred years before was now materialized by a woman in another form.

Well of Concubine Zhen: Fate of Concubine Zhen

Go northward from the Hall of Joyful Longevity to Zhen Shun Men (the Gate of Faith) behind Jing Qi Ge (the Pavilion of Great Happiness) and you will see a low wall half-shaded by some bamboo. Under this low wall, there is a dried-up well, called Zhenfei Jing (Well of Concubine Zhen). Of the numerous stories about the figures in the Imperial Palace, Concubine Zhen ranks among the most well-known. It is only natural that one will not forget to come over here, see the Zhenfei Jing, and ponder over the past.

Well of Concubine Zhen (Concubine Zhen must have been forced into this well of only ten inches in diameter. It is said Concubine Zhen remained as calm as she used to when pulled out of the well, her body un-decayed.)

One day in summer in the 26th year of Guangxu (1900) Empress Dowager Cixi, instead of having a nap as she used to, got up from her bed, acted against her normal behavior to open the curtain by herself, washed her face, and went directly to Yi He Xuan (the Belvedere of Well-nourished Harmony) to the north of the Hall of Joyful Longevity, without taking any maid servant with her. She ordered a eunuch to have Concubine Zhen come out to meet her. The eight-power allied troops were about to attack Beijing and Cixi was planning to run away. She decided to settle the matter, before her departure, once for all with Concubine Zhen.

Two years earlier, the Reform Movement of 1898 had ended in failure. Concubine Zhen, who was so dearly treasured by Guangxu and who was so earnestly in support of Guangxu in his reform movement, became a thorn in the flesh and a sting in the eye of Cixi, and was thus consigned to limbo, confined in a place in the northeast corner of the Ning Shou Gong Area. As recalled an old eunuch, Concubine Zhen was shut in a house full of cobwebs that was frequented by rats and scorpions. A eunuch sent over food once every two or three days, which was handed in through a small opening in the door.

A Portrait of Concubine Zhen (In 1887, Guangxu obeyed Cixi in making her niece his empress, whom he later left in the cold. He stayed partial to Concubine Zhen, and this greatly annoyed Cixi.)

A eunuch had Concubine Zhen taken out of the palace where she was jailed. Then Cixi gave the word: Foreigners were about to invade the city. To avoid insults, Concubine Zhen must finish her own life.

The unyielding concubine retorted in protest and refused to obey, demanding that she meet the emperor. Cixi dismissed the request, and commanded eunuch Cui Yugui to push Concubine Zhen by force into the little well in the Gate of Faith. Concubine Zhen there drowned at the age of only 25.

The next morning, Cixi fled to Xi'an and a year later, survived the inexorable doom, took Guangxu, and returned to Beijing. Until then, the emperor had not learnt that his much-loved wife had died so miserably. However, he could only afford to weep inwardly to himself.

The fate of Concubine Zhen has reflected not only the turbulence of court politics but also the misfortune of the life of those imperial concubines in ancient times. Only a few concubines, as documented in history, were able to win favor from the emperors, and the majority lived a solitary life, killing time as time passed by. They are a special group of women, who deserve compassion. Those, who were specially favored, like Concubine Zhen, by the emperors, might still not be able to be masters of their own fate, and misfortune could befall them at anytime. As a matter of fact, the "ending" as arranged by Cixi for Concubine Zhen is, under some specific circumstances, not uncommon in the history of China. "Death offer" to imperial concubines, with such presentably sound reason as an "offer of help to avoid possible shame or insult by an opponent," became an established custom, especially when the emperors were in despair.

As an appendage of imperial power and politics, the fate of these women, from the day they stepped inside the palace walls, was doomed. Most likely, they would be irreplaceable victims.

A Historic Symphony of Joys and Sorrows

—From Imperial Garden to Jing Hill

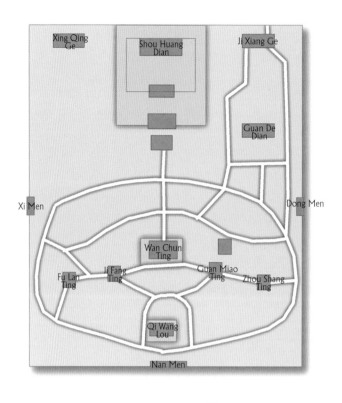

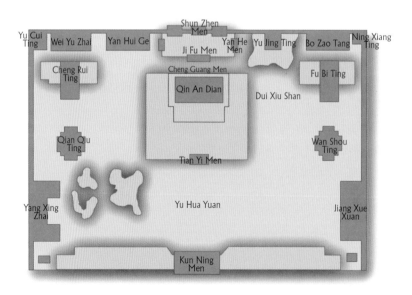

Plan of the Imperial Garden and Jing Hill

Imperial Garden: Back Garden of the Imperial Palace

The Imperial Garden is situated to the north of the Three Rear Palaces. Stand Kun Ning Men (the Gate of Earthly Tranquility), and you can't miss the gorgeous scenery in the garden.

The Imperial Garden was designed and constructed together with the Forbidden City, which used to be called Back Garden of Palace, meaning the back garden of the Imperial Palace. Pine and cypress trees, rare flowers and plants, strange rocks, as well as clear streams are readily found in the garden, which were specially intended for entertainment and appreciation by emperors, empresses, and imperial concubines. Some ceremonial activities like height ascending and full moon enjoyment were performed here each year. Tourists, who have wound up their visit to the front court and the rear palace, may feel a different vitality and sentiment here in this green world of trees and flowers. One can well imagine the ease the emperors experienced here together with their concubines.

The Imperial Garden is after all a back garden of the Forbidden City, which, compared with the ordinary gardens in terms of architecture, is of a special style and excellence of its own. The garden, with its axial and parallel concept of design, is solemn, elegant and soothing, forming a part of the complete whole of the Forbidden City and displaying the character of an imperial court—a real picture of the imperial power and politics.

Tian Yi Men (the First Gate of Heaven) in front of the Hall of Imperial Peace (Each year the emperor would come here to pray to the God of Water so that fires might be kept far away.)

The gardening art as observed in the Imperial Garden is characterized by a combination of such techniques as balance, comparison and contrast, as well as paired association. Importance is also attached to the individuality of each scenic spot, and to variation as opposed to repetition. Visitors may therefore be fascinated by so great a variety and will find it hard to take it all in.

The garden is 80 meters in width from south to north and 140 meters long from east to west. Qian An Dian (the Hall of Imperial Peace), in which the Taoist God is enshrined, is located right in the middle of the garden, with around 20 architectural structures built on the east and the west sides. Wan Chun Ting (the Ten-thousand-spring Pavilion) is symmetrical to Qian Qiu Ting (the Thousand-autumn Pavilion). Both pavilions are topped with round and pyramidal roofs of twelve corners. Fu Bi Ting (the Pavilion of Green Ripples) and the Cheng Rui Ting (the Pavilion of Auspicious Clarity) echo one another from a distance, and both are built on bridges. In addition, the two pavilions are both covered with four-corner pyramidal

The Ten-thousand-spring Pavilion

roofs, with a wing attached to the south. These originally symmetrical structures were not likely to be observed simultaneously as a whole, because of the separation of view by the Hall of Imperial Peace, making the entire space more interesting to view.

Jiang Xue Xuan (the Belvedere of Crimson Snow Flakes) and Yang Xing Zhai (the Room of Spiritual Cultivation) are seated at the southeast corner and the southwest corner of the garden respectively. Of the two structures, one appears convex in shape and the other concave in form, with a difference in height and tone of color. This allows a dynamic vividness amid the symmetry.

Chi Zao Tang (the Hall of Literary Elegance) lies to the north of the Pavilion of Green Ripples, which serves as a stack room for the storage of the Complete Library in the *Four Branches of Literature* collected then by Emperor Qianlong. The Imperial Garden is also full of literary flavor.

The Hall of Literary Elegance is symmetrical to Wei Yu Zhai (Lodge for Proper Places and Cultivation of Things) behind the Pavilion of Auspicious

The Dui Xiu Hill (The concubines, who were not allowed to be out of the palace unless permitted to, would ascend the pavilion to look far towards their own homes, making good wishes to their folks far away.)

Clarity. On the west side of the Hall of Literary Elegance stands, against the wall, an artificial hill formed of rocks in strange shapes, called the Dui Xiu Shan (Hill of Accumulated Elegance or Dui Xiu Hill). On the top of the hill is located a pavilion by the name of Yu Jing Ting (the Imperial Prospect Pavilion), which is higher than the wall of the rear palace, and is, therefore, a good spot for a panoramic view.

The Dui Xiu Hill and Yan Hui Ge (the Pavilion of Prolonged Sunshine), which are symmetrical to the Dui Xiu Hill, separate the garden from the city wall in the north, allowing, in the midst of bewilderment, a fanciful association of range upon range of mountains and meandering streams.

A Distant View of the Forbidden City from the Dui Xiu Hill

There is a gate that leads straight to the Dui Xiu Hill. Behind the gate is a cave and two Chinese characters 堆秀 (*duixiu*) are seen inscribed upon the entrance gate. This is a man-made hill, and was then named Dui Xiu Style. This is where the present name of the hill originates from.

Ascending along the spiral stone steps takes one up to the Imperial Prospect Pavilion on the hilltop, where a view of Xi Shan (the West Hill) comes in sight from afar. Looking down allows a panoramic view of the

Forbidden City. In clear weather, the splendor of a sea of golden-glazed tiled palaces in the south will generously reveal itself under the blue sky.

While taking a brief rest from this vantage point, we can take the opportunity to learn more about the construction of the Forbidden City.

The Forbidden City is about 960 meters long from south to north, and around 750 meters in width from east to west, intersected by some enclosed spaces (courts, complexes and squares), which vary in size for their respective purposes, and consequently contribute to a diversified atmosphere. Walk from the Golden Water Bridge in front of the Gate of Heavenly Peace and you will first see an open square and the tall city towers, creating a wonderful visual excitement. There is a relatively narrower space in between the Gate of Heavenly Peace and the Gate of Uprightness, and when you walk there, you will have a sense of restraint. Across from the Gate of Uprightness unfolds a long narrow space, at the end of which is the Meridian Gate. Splendid as it may look, one finds it hard to dispel the feeling of lifelessness and oppression. Between the Meridian Gate and the Gate of Supreme Harmony lies an extended square, which indeed offers another impressive sight. The magnificent Hall of Supreme Harmony comes into view when you pass through the Gate of Supreme Harmony and enter the square in front of the Hall, which is still yet another stirring visual and emotional experience.

Such contrasting shifts of space are not unusual in the Forbidden City, which stays forever exemplary in the ancient architectural art of China.

The main body of the Forbidden City is of wooden structures. *Nanmu* (a soft wood known as Phoebe *Zhennan*) was mostly used, which was cut and transported from the remote provinces of Yunnan, Guangdong, Hunan and Sichuan. According to the descriptions from earlier generations about the cutting and transporting of wood in the Ming Dynasty, several thousand laborers were hired to move one great timber out of the mountains. A slight tumbling or tilting of the tree could crush a laborer to death. The number of people who could no longer tolerate the unpredicted risk and heavy workload of the shifting of wood and who thus decided to run away in the course of transportation, reached into the tens of thousands. Those who drowned in rivers while transporting the trees by water were equally numerous.

Countless laborers were worked to death or died from diseases at the construction site of the Forbidden City in the Yongle years. To this day, human bones deserted here continue to be unearthed from time to time during the renovations and preservations of the Imperial Palace.

The Forbidden City was built—formed of the wood and rock piled up piece by piece and lump by lump—on the foundation of an autocratic system that functioned by exploiting the rights, freedoms and the lives of other people.

Yet this is true of all the glorious projects that resulted under the rule of imperial power.

Gate of Puisuit of Truth: Selection of Beauty

Three thousand beautiful ladies and ten thousand pretty girls. This is how people in ancient times used to so describe the large number of maids in the empress's palace.

The Gate of Pursuit of Truth (linked to the Imperial Garden, and thus also known as the Garden Gate. Those selected into the palace through this gate lived a life much less beautiful than the garden itself.)

How did so many court maids and imperial concubines come to be in the Imperial Palace? To gather up girls and select the best looking was a normal practice known as "beauty selection."

The Gate of Pursuit of Truth is the entrance one must take from the Imperial Garden to the Gate of Divine Prowess, and this used to be the most frequent location where selection of the beautiful women took place in the Qing Dynasty. Mid-term selection in the Qing Dynasty is documented, and candidates from various parts of the country are described as eventually arrived at Beijing, entering the Gate of Earthly Peace, passing the Gate of Divine prowess before reaching the Gate of Pursuit of Truth, where some officials from Ministry of Revenue divided the candidates up into five-member groups waiting to be selected. After the initial round of selection, a second round took place.

Selection of the best-looking girls was initiated in the Eastern Han Dynasty. Every year, men were sent out to go among ordinary families, searching for nice-looking girls aged between 13 and 20, who were then summoned to the court and waited to be selected. Those bestowed royal favors might go on to become concubines. According to folk legend, Emperor Suiyang would be accompanied by thousands of court maids each time he went out on a tour, and this became typical of the debauchery of an emperor.

The practice of "beauty selection" is an outgrowth of the autocratic imperial power, a concentrated manifestation of the evil and hideousness of privileged politics. Girls to be selected had to undergo a very strict examination procedure, including a close check-up of all the body parts. Those selected into the court would invariably live an unfortunate life. Instances of resentment and rejection to the selection were numerous. Huang Zongxi, thinker of the Ming Dynasty, mercilessly castigated the sacrilegious system, "All this bloodsucking exploitation and family separation is intended only for one man to be indulged in carnal pleasures."

Beauty selection was further enhanced in the Qing Dynasty. The court stipulated that girls of the privileged families of Eight Banners shall not marry prior to the selection (an indication of the preferential possessive right of the imperial court to the womenfolk on earth). At the selection, kneeling was not required (since some of them might be chosen as imperial concubines or even the empress). Some of the selected would be assigned to the rear palaces, and some recommended by the emperor as wives of his sons and grandsons, or wives of the princes and monarchs, or wives of the sons of the princes and monarchs. During the reigns of Tongzhi and Guangxu, all the selected girls would go through another round of selection by the empress dowager, the empress and the imperial concubines for court maids. The emperor became disengaged with such selections. By this time, the "nice-looking" girls were reduced to mere maid servants.

In January of the third year of the reign of Xianfeng, there occurred an instance of rejection by a girl summoned for selection. At that time, the troops of Taiping Heavenly Kingdom were sweeping down from the southeast, and the rule of the Qing court was crumbling. However, Emperor Xianfeng was, as usual, engaged in his selection. That day more than twenty girls were lined up in the Imperial Garden waiting for the selection to start, but Xianfeng really took his time to make his appearance. The girls were cold and hungry, and began to sob. They became even more horrified when the officials began to menace them with whips. Just then a girl stepped forward bravely, accusing with indignation, "We have left our own homes and departed from our own parents. Once we are selected, we shall never meet our folks again. How can we force ourselves not to weep over our misfortune at the thought of our final separation? The Son of Heaven is not thinking of how to fight the rebellion, and is instead obsessed with women, taking possession of them and shutting them up in the palace with force, so that they will never be able to see the blue sky again, all for one day of pleasure for a single man! Are we scared of being whipped when we fear no death?"

It is recounted that Emperor Xianfeng happened to pass by and heard the girl speaking in such seriousness. He gasped in great admiration at so unusual a woman, giving order to the court eunuch to send her back home.

Longevity Hill Refuses to Assure Long Life

Just to the north of the Gate of Divine Prowess and opposite what is

Jing Hill (Its central peak happens to fall on the central axial line of the City of Beijing, and is a vantage point at that. In 1928, the Jing Hill was turned into Jingshan Park.)

today Jing Hill Front Street is a hill, 45.7 meters high. There are five peaks on the top of the hill from east to west, with age-old cypress trees towering high up into the sky, presenting a beautiful scene.

In the Yuan Dynasty, this used to be an artificial hill, known as Qing Hill. Architectural structures like Yan Chun Ge (the Pavilion of Prolonging Spring) are built on the hill, which form part of the Imperial Palace. In the 18th year of Emperor Yongle of the Ming Dynasty, a hill called Zhen Shan (Zhen Hill or Dominating Hill) was piled up using the residual earth from the dismantled palaces of the Yuan Dynasty and the silt of the moat of the Forbidden City. The middle peak happens to be on the former site of the Yan Chun Pavilion. *Zhen* here means to suppress or subdue some force that perishes the kingly way of Yuan Dynasty and impairs the geomancy (a form of divination from the analysis of handfuls of earth). The hill was also named Wan Sui Shan (Longevity Hill) in the hope that the hill would acquire some supernatural power to work miracles and ensure the dynasty remained immutable for all eternity.

Portrait of Emperor Chongzhen

However, the Longevity Hill did not last as long as is expected to. Over two hundred years later, the last emperor Chongzhen committed suicide here on the hill. The state power was again shifted. The Longevity Hill was once a symbol of rise of the Ming Dynasty, but it eventually turned out to be a perilous path to the downfall of the Ming Dynasty. This is quite a miserable scene in the history of the Ming and Qing Dynasties that occurred in March of the 13th year of Chongzhen (1644).

On the 18th of March, the insurrectionary army led by Li Zicheng attacked and captured the City of Beijing. Refusing to give up his throne, Chongzhen first forced Empress Zhou to commit suicide, and arranged to send the prince and other two sons out of the palace before killing his six-year-old daughter Princess Zhaoren and injuring his sixteen-year-old daughter Princess Changping with his sword. While he was stabbing Princess Changping, he yelled loudly, "Why were you born in this family!" Chongzhen also stabbed to death Concubine Yuan, who was not successful in her attempt at suicide, and many other concubines as well.

That night, Chongzhen fled stealthily out of his palace in the pitch dark, but found himself at the end of his rope. He then went back to the palace, and sounded the bell in an attempt to gather up people for a life-or-death resistance. However, no one responded. When dawn came, Chongzhen,

A distant view of the Bell and Drum Towers

in total despair, went up to the Longevity Hill and hanged himself on a pagoda tree at the age of 34. He wrote on his robe, before his death, "My men have betrayed me. I feel too ashamed to face my ancestors. Let the bastards torture my country, but do not hurt my people."

During the reign of Shunzhi of the Qing Dynasty, Longevity Hill was renamed Jing Hill. In the years of Qianlong, the five pavilions on the five peaks were respectively named, from the left to the right, Fu Lan Ting (the Pavilion of Abundant View), Ji Fang Ting (the Pavilion of Assembling Fragrance), the Ten-thousand-spring Pavilion, Guan Miao Ting (the Pavilion of Wonderful View) and Zhou Shang Ting (the Pavilion of Panoramic View). The Ten-thousand-spring Pavilion has a triple-eave pyramidal roof with yellow glazed tiles. Bronze Buddha statues are enshrined in the five pavilions, which were plundered or destroyed by the invaders of the eight-power allied forces.

Jing Hill witnessed the rise and fall of another dynasty after seeing the prosperity and adversity of the Ming Dynasty.

Decline of Imperial Power and the Rebirth of the Imperial Palace

A panoramic view of the City of Beijing is in sight from the Ten-thousand-spring Pavilion of the Jing Hill.

A bird's-eye view of the Gate of Divine Prowess (the northern gate of the Forbidden City, named in the Ming Dynasty as the Xuan Wu Men (the Gate of Genbu), and renamed to avoid the glorious name of Emperor Kangxi; the current front gate of the Palace Museum, welcoming the inflow of numerous visitors everyday)

The Forbidden City in the south with its high and steep palaces is silent without words, but the city moat, with ripples stirred up in the breeze, seems to have something to say.

The big characters "Palace Museum" on the Gate of Divine Prowess, which are hand-inscribed by Guo Moruo, are faintly visible.

Over the last one hundred years, this once heavily guarded and secluded imperial palace is now turned into a museum open to visitors from all over the world. This development is a reflection of the fall of the imperial power politics in China and the rebirth of the nation.

The history of the "opening to the public" of the Forbidden City can be traced back to the year 1900. After the invasion into and the occupation of Beijing by the eight-power allied forces, the military commanders of the United States and Japan formulated a "Regulations on Visits to the

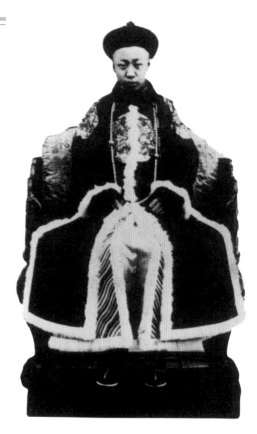

Puyi coming back to his dethroned power (the dethroned Puyi stayed residing in the interior court of the Forbidden City. In 1917, Zhang Xun, a northern warlord was in full support of the restoration of Puyi to power. The farce, however, lasted only for over ten days before its hasty conclusion.)

Forbidden City" composed of eight provisions, of which the third and the fourth stipulate:

Visitors shall be admitted at the south gate and exit from the north gate. The other gates shall all be closed.

No one shall be allowed to enter where a "No Admittance" sign is present.

Five years later, Zhang Jian, a native of Nantong, presented a memorandum to the emperor, suggesting that an Imperial Exposition Hall be established in Beijing and that some of the court collections be moved there and made open to the public. This idea of founding an exposition hall in China originated in the second half of the 19th century, and formed, for a time, an important part of the new policies as advocated by the reformists. The proposal by Zhang Jian materialized the idea, which was later put into practice in his hometown.

However, the suggestion of the establishment of an Imperial Exposition Hall was little heeded. The Qing government was lacking in its ability to cope with the turbulent and changeable situation of the time. A decadent system is like an aged organism, which is unlikely to recuperate and is doomed to destruction.

On November 15 1908, Empress Dowager Cixi, who had been in imperial power for about half a century, passed away. The night before her death, Emperor Guangxu died a sudden death and Cixi designated Puyi, who was then only three years old, to succeed to the throne. Three years later, the Revolution of 1911 announced the end of imperial rule in China. Despite the following farcical attempts to restore the old system, the republican and democratic trends of the times proved irresistible. Those who went against this current were sure be doomed to destruction.

In earlier times the Chinese people habitually called the Imperial Palace the Ancient Palace. After the downfall of the Qing Dynasty, the Forbidden City of Beijing became the Imperial Palace of today. In 1914, the Beijing Municipal Government formed the Antique Exhibition Hall in the Hall of

Puyi regained his power at the Palace of Heavenly Purity in 1917

Literary Brilliance and the Hall of Martial Valor, and decided the collection pieces in the two temporary imperial dwelling places in Liaoning and Rehe be stored in the two halls. Lu Xun once took his friend to pay a visit there. In 1925, the formation of the Palace Museum was officially initiated, and on October 10 of the same year, a grand opening ceremony took place.

On that Double-ten Holiday, crowds of people poured into what used to be the Forbidden City. As reported, "People in Beijing emptied their lanes on the National Day, swarming into this mysterious land of several thousand years old, hoping to have a peek at its wonders. People were ambling along, looking around, and talking and laughing among themselves." The socialization of the Palace and its treasures is regarded as a significant progress in the course of the democratic revolution and the formation of a modern social system ever since the Revolution of 1911.

The formation of the Palace Museum marks the rebirth of the Imperial Palace and a major step of the Chinese nation towards the world, democracy, freedom and prosperity.

Xia Dynasty	2070 BC – 1600 BC
Shang Dynasty	1600 BC – 1046 BC
Zhou Dynasty	1046 BC – 256 BC
Western Zhou Dynasty	1046 BC – 771 BC
Eastern Zhou Dynasty	770 BC – 256 BC
Spring and Autumn Period	770 BC – 476 BC
Warring States Period	475 BC – 221 BC
Qin Dynasty	221 BC – 206 BC
Han Dynasty	206 BC – 220 AD
Western Han Dynasty	206 BC – 25 AD
Eastern Han Dynasty	25 AD – 220 AD
Three Kingdoms	220 AD – 280 AD
Wei	220 AD – 265 AD
Shu Han	221 AD – 263 AD
Wu	222 AD – 280 AD
Jin Dynasty	265AD – 420AD
Western Jin Dynasty	265 AD – 316 AD
Eastern Jin Dynasty	317 AD – 420 AD
Northern and Southern Dynasties	420 AD – 589 AD
Southern Dynasties	420 AD – 589 AD
Northern Dynasties	439 AD – 581 AD
Sui Dynasty	581 AD – 618 AD
Tang Dynasty	618 AD – 907 AD
Five Dynasties and Ten States	907 AD – 960 AD
Five Dynasties	907 AD – 960 AD
Ten States	902 AD – 979 AD
Song Dynasty	960 AD – 1279
Northern Song Dynasty	960 AD – 1127
Southern Song Dynasty	1127 – 1279
Liao Dynasty	916 AD – 1125
Jin Dynasty	1115 – 1234
Xixia Dynasty	1038 – 1227
Yuan Dynasty	1279 – 1368
Ming Dynasty	1368 – 1644
Qing Dynasty	1644 – 1911